3—

NATIVE AMERICAN HUNTING AND FIGHTING
SKILLS

NATIVE AMERICAN
HUNTING AND FIGHTING
SKILLS

Colin F. Taylor

THE LYONS PRESS

A SALAMANDER BOOK

Published in the United States by
The Lyons Press
Guilford, CT 06437.
www.lyonspress.com
The Lyons Press is an imprint of The Globe Pequot Press.

© Salamander Books Ltd 2003

A member of **Chrysalis** Books plc

ISBN 1-58574-705-X

1 2 3 4 5 6 7 8 9 10

Credits
Editor: Marie Clayton
Designer: Cara Hamilton
Reproduction: Anorax Imaging Ltd
Printed in China

Acknowledgements
It is a pleasure to acknowledge the input of a number of individuals who have been willing to give opinions relating to the various topics covered in this volume. I turned to Colonel (Retd.) John Bennett and Major (Retd.) Rodney Turner, for observations on military (and related hunting) strategies, as well as ballistics. Fraser Lakes generously shared his own researches on North American Indian warfare. Major Kevin Galvin, Neil Gilbert, Barry Johnson and Francis Taunton (all members of The English Westerners' Society), made several, very useful thought-provoking observations relating to the Indian–White confrontations of the nineteenth century. Insights relating to the reasons for developing various styles of hunting and warfare skills, have been gained by discussions and travel with Sam Cahoon, Hugh and Pauline Dempsey, the late John C. Ewers, Mike Johnson and Ian West. Others who have helped in various ways are Kingsley Bray, Scott Burgen, Dagmara Ginter, Ned and Judy Martin, John Painter, Carl Sun and Putt Thompson.
Thanks also to the production staff of Chrysalis Books and to my wife, Betty, for her usual support in all projects of this sort.

Contents

Introduction

Below right: One of the earliest forms of Peace Medal. This is associated with William Penn (1644–1718), founder of the state of Pennsylvania. The medal was struck in 1757 and given to chiefs at the settlement of Shamokin, to show the benevolent and friendly intentions of the settlers towards the Delaware, Shawnee and Iroquois. The Indians referred to Penn as "Brother Onas," and he is shown offering the calumet of peace to a chief. The calumet points towards the sun and is said to be symbolic of both the purity and durability of friendship between the nations.

This is a companion volume to *Native American Weapons* (Taylor, Salamander, 2001) which was a broad overview of weapons used by the North American Indians in both war and hunting. That volume created considerable discussion, not only with the Military Book Clubs but also by members of the American and British forces, undoubtedly due to the increasing interest in American Indian warfare tactics, a number of which had parallels in hunting. Because of the obvious overlap between war and hunting—weapons used, tactics employed—this volume has extended the study to include both themes.

Although it attempts to contrast and evaluate tactics and strategies used in North America, more consideration is given to the Woodlands, Southwest and the Great Plains.

One major thrust is the Plains region, for which we have extensive data scattered through the literature. It was the home to many groups who moved in

from other cultural areas. Initially employing tried and tested techniques inherited from their original homelands, they quickly adapted and changed to match new conditions.

Not least, this study considers the changing military and hunting patterns and skills under the impact of the gun, horse and white encroachment. The whole is a fascinating, and at times tragic, saga of both continuity and change.

Sources have been carefully documented throughout the text. One particular volume that I found of great value and interest was Malone's (1991) studies relating to warfare of the Indians of New England. Few detailed studies have been made of Native American warfare and hunting tactics, much of the data being scattered through the literature. This volume attempts to bring together some of this disparate material. No claims are made that it is exhaustive; it is a vast topic.

Some of those who were confronted on the battlefield, or intimately involved with the American Indian, have left useful and rewarding firsthand accounts; Custer, Bourke, Crook, *et al*, for the Plains and Southwest immediately spring to mind. But earlier observers, such as Governor John Winthrop and Roger Williams—who were involved in the Pequot Wars of the 1640s—have left priceless records.

Another valuable description of warfare skills was by the Cree chief, *Saukamappee*. He documented much, based on firsthand experience of hostile encounters between Blackfeet and Shoshone in the early eighteenth century. Related hunting skills were documented by such observers as George Catlin, and the trader Edwin Denig, in the early to mid-nineteenth century,

Leading on from studies, such as those by Marquis (1931), have been the publishing of Indian accounts relating to the Indian Wars (Greene, 1994, and Hardorff, 1995), underlining an increasing interest in such matters. The study of strategies and tactual skills in the hunt and war have, however, received only limited attention.

Terrain and Environment

Terrain and environment clearly had a considerable impact on hunting and warfare. To take extreme cases, the heavily wooded forests of the Northeast required considerably different strategies for survival than for those groups who lived in the deserts and oft-barren environments of the Southwest and Great Basin region.

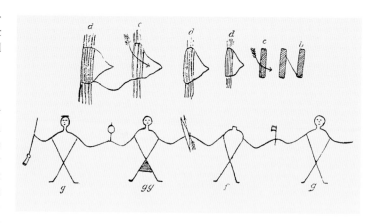

The need for stealth of movement, however, was a common factor throughout most regions and the ploy of the decoy was common. Even the "pound technique" (see below), so favored by the Woodland and Plains, was practised by the Great Basin people—for grasshoppers!

Although the bow was also widely used, forested regions obscured the flight of the arrow and the hunter or warrior needed to get particularly close to his quarry in order to make a kill. On the Plains, or in the desert, this was less crucial, although the curved flight of the arrow and its relative slowness (in comparison to the Atlatl and later the gun), made it less effective than such hunting methods as the "pound." In the latter, hundreds of animals—caribou, antelope, deer and buffalo—could be killed in one skillfully coordinated hunt, close to the herds. Likewise in warfare where, in early days prior to the introduction of the horse and gun, close hand warfare with club, spear or knife was far more effective than firing arrows or hurling lances at distant opponents. (Chapter IV)

Above: *Iroquois pictographs of martial exploits. "f" is a warrior killed, "gg" a woman captured.*

Below: *A Huron deer drive; the pound could extend for half a mile.*

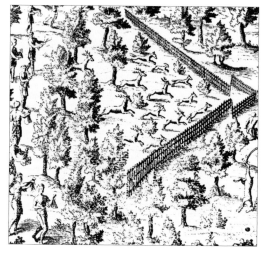

The impact of the gun and horse

The gun, and in several instances the horse, changed many of the well-tried techniques. As discussed in Chapters II and IV, the availability of the gun to kill or cripple game or enemy at a distance not only initially filled the Indians with awe, but also caused a dramatic change in their strategies and tactics. Body armor, for example, used widely throughout North America and effective against indigenous weaponry, was soon discarded (perhaps replaced by a symbolic garment or emblem).

Gun-armed tribes now expanded their territories—the Mohawk quickly subjugating the Lenni Lenape and expanding their territory; later, a number of Algonquian and Siouan tribes were driven onto the Plains by gun-armed Chippewa.

On the Plains, Piegan, using muskets (c.1740) caused consternation amongst the equestrian, but only bow-armed, Shoshone. The "deadly aim" of the Piegan caused the Shoshone to take flight.

The natural ready comprehension, sharp perception and coordination of the Native American warrior soon led to great skill with the gun and its proficient use in the war and hunt. It was increasingly rec-

Below: The "still hunt," as practiced by the Plains Indians, after a painting by George Catlin, c.1833. Here, the hunters are dressed in wolf skins and are approaching the herd stealthily. Healthy buffalo were not intimidated by wolves, who often followed the herd to prey on weak or young animals. A variant of the still hunt was later adapted by white hunters, using guns. (see Chapter VI).

ognized—particularly after the introduction of the flintlock in the mid-1650s—that this weapon was vastly superior to any weapon of their own manufacture. Tribes that had ready access to guns increasingly dominated; the Shoshone and Kutenai, for example, were driven permanently from their long-held homelands, the Northern Plains, and retreated to the Plateau.

Gun and horse together changed warfare and hunting tactics dramatically. Former pedestrians, armed with bow or spear, now moved rapidly on horseback. The old infantry-style warfare, outmoded slow movement, was particularly dangerous against the gun. Skills on horseback—dropping behind the horse to use it as a shield, surrounding buffalo, "circling" the white enemy to draw fire and then make a quick kill (Chapter VI), were now carefully practised.

However, a major limitation was the ready and reliable availability of gun and ammunition. It is well recorded that Indians were proficient in the repair of guns and they could also mold musket balls. One vital technology lacking, however, was the manufacture of gunpowder. (Chapter II)

Recycling of weapons was also practised; thus broken and discarded guns used by white soldiers in the Rosebud fight were repaired by the Oglala warrior, Good Hand, who "knew how to make them work very well, even those the soldiers had broken whipping their horses." (Sandoz, 1961:322) Broken weapons and tools might also be recycled for other purposes; the receiver of a Yellow Boy (a military piece) was skillfully employed by a Comanche craftsman—as a hammer when making arrowheads! (p.11) As Crazy Horse said, "Nothing must be forgotten when iron is so scarce." (ibid:323)

As Chapter III records, for the Apache hunting and warfare skills were only acquired by hard practise and dedication. The

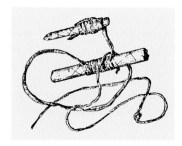

Above: *An Apache scratch stick and drinking reed. These were used by young Apache warriors as part of the warpath ritual. (see Chapter III)*

Below: *The Pueblo of Taos, in present-day New Mexico, built on the slopes of a high plateau at the base of a sacred mountain. Partially fortified, it was the scene of many intertribal conflicts over a period of more than one thousand years.*

"novice complex" was well developed by several Southern Athapascan groups, such as the Tonto, Cibecue, San Carlos and White Mountain Apaches. Sustained endurance, so important for survival in the hostile terrain of Apache territory, was only acquired by hard training. Boys were encouraged at a young age to hunt animals and small birds and to participate in sham battles. When taken on the warpath as helpers, there were various taboos that forbad letting water directly touch the lips and special sticks had to be used when scratching the head. (p.10) It instilled a rigorous discipline and vigilance—and made skilled, efficient hunters and formidable warriors.

Unlike the professional soldier, the majority of North American Indian males were part-time warriors, but full-time providers. Clearly, there was a desire to keep casualties to a minimum, otherwise the social structure of the small population societies would be destroyed. As one scholar has said in the case of the Iroquois, their mode of warfare suited their society and "If pressed hard, they normally retreated." (Benn, 1998:80)

The strong relationship between hunting and warfare skills has also been emphasized for the Iroquois. Analyses of the conditions to assess numbers, condition of the ground to assess the length of time since they left the spot, and tactics such as surrounding the quarry, stealth, ambush and confusing rapid movement—these were all techniques commonly employed in both hunt and war. (ibid:76-79) They were not unique to the Iroquois—they were skills widely used throughout North America.

Whilst in such a compact volume we can only consider a "snap shot" of these subjects, an attempt has been made to look at some aspects of hunting and war in depth. The author has also tried to identify the various skills that were common, or unique, to both activities: all vital to the North American Indian lifeway.

Below: A Comanche arrowhead-making kit, showing the heads in various stages of completion. Of particular interest here is that the receiver of a gun (top) has been recycled as a hammer, to shape the metal heads. (Courtesy Ned and Jody Martin Collection, Hallack Creek Valley)

CHAPTER I

Waku'wapi kte

("To/ shall pursue" - Lakota)

The Way of Hunting
& War in North America

"We knew the habits of the different kinds of birds [and animals] and that each kind had its own feeding grounds where we could find them"
Goodbird (Hidatsa)(Gilman & Schneider, 1987:70).

Right: *The atlatl, or spear thrower. Some 18 inches (45cm) in length, this device effectively added an extra joint and extension to the arm. It thus increased the efficiency of the hurl, and increased momentum was gained by attaching a stone weight to the end. It was used for thousands of years in North America and before the advent of the bow. It was a lethal weapon, for both hunting and warfare, in skilled hands.*

FROM THE ARCTIC REGIONS of the far north to the deserts of the southwest, from the lake and forested areas of the east to the rugged terrain and sea of the west coast, the Native Americans efficiently and skillfully extracted a living from their environment.

As with all hunters throughout the world the North American

Indian needed to be well versed in the variety of processes and techniques which enabled him to trap and secure the quarry—be it fish, fowl or mammal.

Not infrequently such environments were hostile, dangerous and unpredictable, but by great skill coupled with tenacity, courage and intelligence most Native American groups lived well.

Honed so finely, the essential hunting abilities were often extrapolated to the field of war. Thus, skills with the atlatl (later the bow), the lance or spear and the dextrous use of the knife or tomahawk were all put to good use in both defensive and offensive warfare.

Foremost in the hunt was the appropriate selection of traps, pits, snares or weapons which matched the task in hand. A detailed knowledge of the animals' behavioral patterns was also essential, thus enabling calls, whistles, decoys or hiding places to be effectively employed.

A good knowledge of the pursued quarry's anatomy was also important—in order to know where to strike and so to efficiently kill and butcher.[1] Associated with all these activities were hunting rituals and taboos, which often entailed elaborate ceremonial, song and (sometimes) dance.[2]

Every technique of hunting—as in war—taxed the ingenuity of the Native American. Not least was a careful consideration of mode of travel and transportation. Thus, in order to use a harpoon on a fast moving quarry such as a whale or salmon, it was necessary to have a sleek light-weight kayak or canoe. In order to stalk a deer a Woodland hunter needed tightly fitting leggings and soft-soled moccasins—both of which ensured the essential stealth of movement. In more extreme conditions, such as the pursuit of a moose in heavy snow, the moccasined feet required the support of snowshoes. Farther north the boot-like mukluk of the Inuit replaced the moccasin: perhaps more

Above: *A Nootka whaler with harpoon. The harpoon was up to 18 feet (6m) in length and generally made of yew wood. The point was of sharp mussel shell, with elk horn barbs. An inflated sealskin, attached to the shaft, impeded the dive of the whale after the first strike and subsequently acted as a buoy. These whalers were hereditary chiefs. During the hunt, they occupied a position in the bow of the canoe.*

Above: Inuit hunters examining a bow. Note scenes of the hunt painted on the bow back.

Below: A motif worked in porcupine quills on a Sioux(?) blanket strip. Traditionally such designs referred to a buffalo pound.

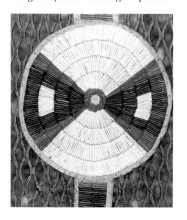

than any other form of footwear in North America, the immensely tough but flexible and waterproof mukluk, was a masterpiece in the highly efficient use of natural materials.

The Nootka whale hunt: a study in skill and ingenuity.

The economy of the Northwest Coast was similar to that of adjacent parts of the Arctic, Subarctic, California and the Western Plateau. Primarily it depended on fish—such as salmon, halibut and sea mammals. A dramatic activity of the coastal tribes, however, was the sea hunt for whales. It was a skill particularly perfected by the Nootka of Vancouver Island employing many of the essential components of the Native American Hunting Complex—as outlined earlier.

Perhaps more than any other hunting mode it underscores the attribute of courage so essential in the make-up of a skilled hunter or for that matter an efficient warrior. It is also a study of self-imposed commitment by a key member of the whaling crew—the harpooner.

The training of a Nootka harpooner generally began at an early age. Essential was the ability to dive and swim in deep icy water, frequently imitating the actions of the whale—rolling and plunging. The would-be whaler, however, also required more than mere human ability. Thus, during a vigil, perhaps after a vigorous day's training, the aspirant sought the support of a supernatural helper. Successful communication was seen as signaling spiritual support and it gave the youth confidence that he could, with further effort, become a successful whaler.[3]

Now the young man began to acquire skills with the harpoon. Experienced men taught him the quickness and alertness needed when facing a whale on the open sea.

The skill of the harpooner was vital. His carefully designed weapon was up to 18 feet (6m) in length, with a detachable head of carved elk horn in which was set a razor-sharp point of mussel shell. On striking the whale the head separated from the shaft, a nettlecord and sinew lanyard connected to the head prevented its escape. When the wounded whale resurfaced more harpoons were plunged into its massive body. The exhausted mammal was finally despatched with a special chisel-head lance.

Clearly such bloody hunts required immense skill and courage on the part of the whalers and it is little wonder that they also evoked the support of supernatural powers!!

These great whale hunts epitomize the battle of man against nature in the Native Americans' efforts to tap nature's bountiful resources for survival.[4]

The Chipewyan caribou hunt

As with the Indians of the Plains and the buffalo, there was a close affinity between the tribes of the Subarctic and the caribou which roamed the tundra —often referred to as the Barren Grounds—in countless thousands.[5] The caribou was essential to the sustainment of life amongst such tribes as the Athapascan speaking Chipewyan.[6] This was a land where the people had a high dependency on the snowshoe in order to fully exploit the natural resources of the region.

The whole material culture of the Chipewyan pivoted on the products attained from the caribou. The hide, antler and bone providing "clothing, bedding, and lodge coverings, and also the babiche (rawhide thong) used for bow strings, snowshoe lacing, gill nets, tumplines, drum-heads, and other objects." (Smith, Helm ed. 1981:280)[7]

The method of hunting the caribou resembled the "pound" technique used by the Plains tribes for the antelope and buffalo, as described in Chapter VI. (Taylor, 1997:111) The hunt was communal

Above: *Kutchin warriors and hunters c.1850. Their clothing is of caribou skin decorated with trade beads and dentalium shells. The man on the right has a bow and arrows, the other a trade flintlock, powder horn and shot pouch. Note the gun's protective covering— essential in the cold of the Arctic.*

in nature, the caribou being driven into the mouth of a chute made of poles or brush. At the appropriate moment concealed men, women and children drove the terrified creatures towards the circular enclosure at the end of the chute. Within the enclosure—which could be over a quarter of a mile in diameter—were skillfully made and placed looped snares. The entangled caribou were then despatched with arrows, spears and clubs.

On occasions the movements of the caribou herds were erratic or unusual. Aware of this, and in order to make the essential kill for survival, there was a complex network of communication between all the scattered Chipewyan bands. One distinguished Subarctic anthropologist was so impressed with the skill

efficiency of this interband organization that he was led to record, "Although in a severe environment, the Chipewyan do not have myths and legends which emphasize starvation." (Smith, 1978:68)[8]

Capturing powers: the eagle and bear hunt

Sustenance alone was not the only motivation for the hunt, the beauty and power of such creatures as the vulture, eagle and bear being widely recognized by the Native Americans—sentiments which were clearly held for aeons.[9]

Birds of prey—the hawk, eagle and vulture—all lent their plumage for clothing, war decorations and ceremonial. Paramount was the eagle which was universally regarded as a majestic bird endowed with a mysterious and mystical nature. Solitary by nature it soared

Above: Wapella *or "Chief,"* *headman of the Musquakee or Fox* *tribe. Described as a man of great* *strength and activity, he was in a* *delegation to Washington in 1837.* *It was there that this portrait was* *produced.* Wapella *displays all the* *trappings of a successful hunter and* *warrior—bear claw necklace, deer* *hair headdress, bearskin cape and* *eagle feathers.*

high above earthbound man and was, in much tribal mythology, related to the awesome Thunderbird. Eagle feathers were valuable trade items and whilst some tribes[10] kept eagles and other birds of prey in captivity (and so ensured an abundant supply of feathers) others hunted them. Some of the most skilled of the eagle hunters were the Mandan and Hidatsa tribes of the Missouri River region. The hunting was generally carried out in the autumn, special eagle traps being used. This was a pit in the ground and just deep enough for the trapper to sit upright. It was covered with a matting of brush on which was placed a meat bait. When the eagle alighted, the hunter grasped one leg with his right hand pulling it down towards the ground. Then the other leg was grasped, the two quickly forced together and held with the left hand. The wings were then forced against each other with the right hand and the tips firmly held. It was a dangerous business. As one experienced eagle hunter advised a novice, "Eagles are strong and fierce. They can stick their claws through your hand, pick your face, or cut your face with their wings." He then added—perhaps somewhat wryly—"Don't catch bald-headed eagles; they are [very] fierce and will fight [even harder]." (Bowers, 1950:246)

The most prized feathers were those from the immature golden eagle. Those from the tail were white with dark brown tips. Sometimes referred to as the "calumet eagle", such feathers made the finest of warbonnets for the successful warrior.

Eagle trapping was carried out with much associated ceremonial. Amongst the Mandan and Hidatsa there were special eagle-trapping Medicine Bundles and certain individuals received "popular recognition comparable to specialists in any other pursuit such as warfare or hunting." (ibid:214) These men inherited with the Bundle, associated hunting territory, the conical hunting lodge (comparable to the war lodge —see Chapter V) and the eagle-trapping pit. Used for a short time annually, it was only necessary to repair and clean them. The lodge was considered a holy

Below: *Mandan buffalo dance. This is a detail from a painting produced by the Swiss artist Karl Bodmer. Bodmer witnessed such scenes at the Minnetaree village in November 1833. Buffalo had been seen in the vicinity of the village and the dance was given to "implore the blessing of heaven." (Thomas and Ronnefeldt eds., 1976:180) During the ceremonial, various chiefs made extensive speeches, expressing good wishes for success in hunt and war.*

Above: *Detail of bow and arrows carried by a Mandan warrior in the buffalo dance. (see picture p.17)*

Below: *A full grown grizzly bear was a formidable opponent.*

enclosure, it housed a buffalo skull altar, the Medicine Bundle, and other sacred accoutrements. These were considered to give spiritual help and protection to the eagle hunter. As with so many activities of the Native American, earthly skills were seldom deemed sufficient to ensure success in hazardous ventures.

Hunting the mighty grizzly

The majestic eagle was linked to that of the bear in Mandan and Hidatsa mythology. It was said that in times gone by, bears trapped young golden eagles. This expertise was brought to the Mandan by one of their culture heroes, Black Wolf, who had been befriended by the bears and taught by them how to trap the eagle. Bear and eagle were thus linked in the minds of the Mandan. (ibid:215) The bear was considered by many tribes as a traditional and greatly admired ancestor; it was the embodiment of all virile virtues which the Native American male aspired to—"strength, courage, and cold belligerence." (McCracken, 1957:27) The chief thing in life was to be brave, "to be brave is what makes a man... do not fear anything... go up close to your enemy. As you charge, you must be saying to yourself all the time, 'I will be brave; I will fear nothing.'" (Grinnell, 1920:38) As one student of the grizzly observed, "the grizzly bear was the personification of all this, and he was more." (McCracken, 1957:27)

Killing such formidable creatures was no easy task.[11] The adult grizzly could weigh up to almost 1000 lbs. (453 kg) and when fully standing was 8 feet (2.4 m) or more. It was seemingly fearless of any other living thing and, depending on its mood or circumstances, might attack on sight. In days when the Native American was armed only with a bow or spear the grizzly viewed humans with indifference—on occasions, however, such apparent disdain was fatal. Many tribes—particularly those of the Plains and Woodlands—had elaborate bear ceremonies which gave recognition to supernatural powers possessed by that animal. Individuals who acquired such powers were considered as blessed to be successful healers or war leaders. These beliefs were widespread and ancient, such as the Huron woman who dreamed of bear power and, hence, organized a bear dance in the hope that it would cure her sickness. An Ottawa war leader used bear power as war medicine! Superior intelligence and the likeness of the bear was delineated on the prow of his canoe. Widespread on the Central and Northern Plains were Bear Cults which gave emphasis to healing and aggressive participation in war expeditions. (Ewers, 1968:131–145)[12]

The Assiniboin hunted bears in winter, locating the den where the bear was in hibernation. Several hunters co-ordinated their efforts firing the first shots, others holding them in reserve. The bear was, thus, progressively weakened and ultimately brought down. (Denig, 1930:538)

Confrontation and victory by single hunters was rare, but on occasion it happened. Little wonder that high-ranking individuals wore the claws of "the beast that walks like man" (*Ursus horribilis*) (McCracken, 1957:13) as a statement of their prowess and success on the battlefield.

Native American Militarism
Winning battles but losing the war
The "classic" concept of war—defeat of a people and an imposition of the will of the victor on the losers—was largely alien to the Native Americans. Early European warfare, which was brought to North America by the colonists, put emphasis on driving the enemy from his position and then exploiting success by inflicting all possible damage on the defeated.[13]

In contrast, the Native Americans only infrequently followed up success in battle. Within a short time after the conflict they generally withdrew and disbanded. As one scholar in this field observed, the Indian "won a lot of battles but lost the war... he did not destroy enemies but treated them more like game."[14] Thus, rather than annihilate, the underlying ethos of Native American militarism related more to revenge, honor, counting coup, acquiring horses, stealing property and taking prisoners.

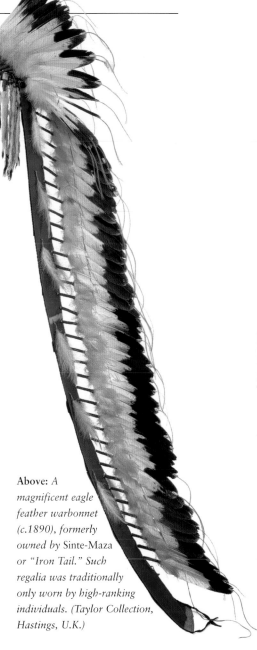

Above: *A magnificent eagle feather warbonnet (c.1890), formerly owned by* Sinte-Maza *or "Iron Tail." Such regalia was traditionally only worn by high-ranking individuals. (Taylor Collection, Hastings, U.K.)*

Winning battles and the war

There were, however, some notable exceptions in Native American militarism which did at times approach the European tenets of war. Not surprisingly, these had far-reaching consequences. Thus, the progressive movement of Algonquian and Siouan tribes to the Northern and Central Plains and the Athapascans and (later) Shoshonean tribes to the Southern Plains displaced the ancient inhabitants to less desirable terrain. The Algonquians and Siouans had in turn been driven westward by gun-armed Chippewa. There were some devastating encounters in the quest for more bountiful protein resources. (Taylor, 1994:14–18)

Similarly in the Great Lakes region and eastwards. Here, a major motive was acquisition of the rich fur-bearing areas of the Canadian Shield—and so profit from the lucrative beaver trade. In the 1640s, the Iroquois began systematically raiding Huron villages and razing them to the ground.[15] By 1649 all the villages east of Sainte Marie had been abandoned, remnants of the Huron joining such tribes as the Neutral, Erie and Ottawa. Others were adopted by the Iroquois: it was a planned destruction of the Huron as an independent tribe.[16]

Destructive warfare of this type was, as has been mentioned earlier, unusual with stable Native American communities. It was widely recognized that aggression (such as that which might be waged by the schemes of ambitious men) could have a socially disintegrating effect and violate ancient teaching. For example, the concept of war amongst the Omaha was allied to the cosmic forces and said to be under their control. These forces were considered to be manifested in the destructive power of the lightning and the "roar of thunder."

Above: A fine Great Lakes sash, probably dating from before 1800. White and red imitation glass-wampum beads are woven together with woolen yarn. The pattern is obviously symbolic. The human figure may make reference to treaty or some ceremonial, between two separate parties. (Courtesy John Painter Collection, Cincinnati)

(Fletcher and LaFlesche, 1911:402) A violation of the will of the God of War could bring his wrath to bear on the offending individual. Consequently, tribal philosophy clearly moderated the character of aggressive warfare in the Omaha mind and was a means of establishing and maintaining tribal control over such activities. The evidence suggests that similar beliefs were held in other cultural areas of North America.

Following the warpath

Although theoretically any man was free to organize and lead an aggressive war-party, in reality the task was generally assumed by experienced individuals. Such individuals conformed to the tribal teachings which were discussed in council and the views of the tribal intellectuals sought.

As one observer of the Ottawa reported in the early 1700s when war was contemplated, the chances of success were carefully weighed. Consideration of the dangers to both warpath members and the community at large were paramount. This was vital in order to conserve precious lives on which the relatively small tribe depended for survival. (Kinietz, 1940:245 –254) Only then could aggressive warfare be sanctioned and the powers of the various Gods of War evoked to ensure success.

Stealthy approach— lightning strike

At daybreak on 29 August 1833 the occupants of Fort McKenzie, a remote trading post on the Upper Missouri, were rudely awakened by the crack of a musket shot. It was the start of a savage intertribal battle much of which was typical of the aggressive warfare tactics of the Plains tribes.

Below: *Return of the warriors, from a painting by Charles M. Russell, 1906. Successful war-parties generally made camp, before entering the village. Here, they rehearsed their victory songs and war exploits. Then, dressed and painted, they rode into the village singing a common war song.*

Fort McKenzie was situated in the very heart of Blackfeet territory.[17] Here bands of Northern Plains Indians—Cree, Assiniboin, Blackfeet—came to trade.

Some twenty tipis of Piegan, a Blackfeet tribe, had been pitched near the Fort. Without warning, they were attacked by a combined force of some six hundred Assiniboin and Cree warriors. The Piegan warriors, vastly outnumbered, gallantly attempted to protect the retreat of the women and children. Some were armed with muzzle-loading flintlocks, others with bows, lances and various forms of war clubs and knives. Within a short time reinforcements began to arrive from the main Piegan camp some eight miles away. Now virtually matched man for man, the furious Piegan drove the enemy back.[18]

This battle illustrates much which was typical of Native American warfare: stealthy approach, lightning strike and rapid withdrawal. Manoeuvres varied somewhat depending on the area, but the element of surprise so as to maximize kill or capture, and then swiftly make off, was universal. Such tactics were largely derived from the methods of hunting where the spoils were generally limited and the outcome did not completely destroy the game that they preyed on. Clearly, the weaponry and techniques for both hunting and war had much in common. Not surprisingly then, exploits of battle and chase were not infrequently rendered on the same pictographic record.

The hunting and war lodge
Perhaps one of the best illustrations of the overlap of war and hunting and the associated strategies adopted is the use of the war and hunting lodge of the Plains tribes. A number of these structures are still to be found in remote parts of the Dakotas and Montana.

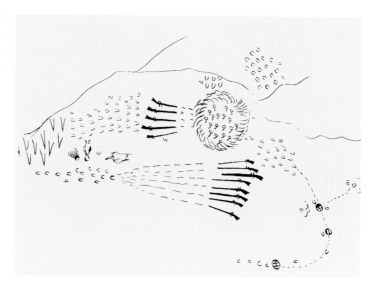

Above: *Assiniboin battle ground, c.1850. Rifle pit, horse hoof prints and flintlocks pictographically document a stirring episode.*

Below: *An early war or hunting lodge, in a remote region of Montana, 1969. (see text)*

Above: *Mandan/Minnetaree warriors in a buffalo dance, detail from a painting by Karl Bodmer. (see p.17) The main figure is firing a flintlock trade musket; to his left is a dancer in buffalo-horn headdress.*

That shown on p.22 is clearly of considerable antiquity. More than sixty years ago Blackfeet informants described the use of such structures to the Plains ethnologist John Canfield Ewers. He reported that they were vital bases for both hunting and war in Plains Indian culture and that they served at least five uses. Not only did they provide protection from the weather but the structure of the lodge provided a strong defensive position. It served as a base for scouting operations and as a supply base. Another important function was as an information station for communication of intelligence amongst members of the war or hunting party. (see Chapter V:87–88) Here, tactics could be discussed and messages (pictographic in form) obtained. Ewers concluded that the architecture suggested that such structures originated in the Northern Woodlands. (Ewers, 1968:129) It is, thus, probable that the concept of the war and hunting lodge had a far wider distribution than has been deduced to date.[19]

It is clear, therefore, that once underway most successful war-parties were well planned. Careful consideration was given to strategies, tactics and chain of command. Intelligence gathering and communication techniques were also worked out. Coupled with this were the issues of the best methods of defence, the best method of attack and the importance of reserves and replein.

Obvious too was the nature of the rewards—slaves, horses, hostages, pillage and, of course, war honors to be gained.

To date, much of this has been largely ignored in the study of the skills employed in Native American warfare with an overemphasis on "the individualistic aspects of warfare." (ibid:129) As the following chapters further demonstrate the militarism which was almost everywhere in tribal societies, was invariably a well-structured and carefully thought out activity of the North American Indian.[20]

CHAPTER II

Nin zon gidee

("I am strong hearted" - Chippewa)

The Stealth & Ethos of Hunt & War: Eastern North America

"[It was] done so well—with slow, and measured steps, and to the rhythmic sound of the voices and drums—that it might pass for a very fine entry of a Ballet in France."

(Dablon, c. 1670 in Mark, 1988:218)

Right: *The main tribes of Florida, when first observed by Europeans in the early 1500s, were the Timucua, Calusa and Apalachee. They were led by powerful chiefs, whose war expeditions might consist of many hundreds of warriors. The death of an individual of high status, such as a religious or war leader, evoked complex funeral ceremonial. Men and women fasted, cutting their hair or drawing blood, to mourn. Shown here is the grave of such an individual, surrounded by a protective ring of arrows and with the mount surmounted by his conch shell water dipper.*

FOR HUNDREDS, if not thousands, of years such pre-war ritual was practiced by the North American Indians. More than two hundred years prior to Dablon's observation, the Spanish had witnessed pre-war ceremonial but little understood the significance of the actions.

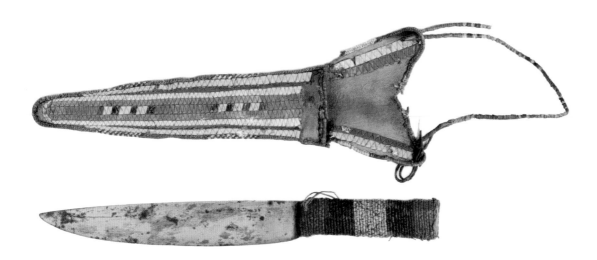

Thus, in 1513, when the Spanish explorer Ponce de Leon attempted to land on the southern shores of present-day Florida, the indigenous Calusa made such a **show** of arms—boldly moving towards the Spanish fleet in eighty canoes—that the Spaniards retreated and thus forfeited the opportunity of forging friendly contacts. The ways of war of Europeans and American Indians were markedly different and tactics on both sides were subsequently modified, as the clash between cultures progressed.[1]

Warfare tactics

The early English in Virginia, clearly viewed Indian warfare tactics with some disdain, one observer recording "that [they] were not acquainted with books of military Discipline, that observe no regular Order, that understand not the Souldier's Postures, and Motions, and Firings, and Forms of Battel, that fight in a base, cowardly, contemptible way." (Lepore, 1998:113) What the colonist, however, failed to fully recognize was that their Indian opponents had their own laws of war, which took firmly into account the nature of the terrain and weaponry available and obviously did not, at this time, include the use of fire power.

That the Woodland tribes carefully planned their military actions,

Above: Sharp-edged stone blades were the precursors of metal knives in North America. Although some copper was worked by the Indians of the Great Lakes and south into the Mississippi valley, it was not until the introduction of trade knives in the 1600s that steel blades began to replace stone and copper. These blades were often sold without handles. Shown here is an early example (c.1800), which is identified as Ojibwa. The handle is decorated with a wrapping of braided porcupine quills. The thin steel blade may qualify it as a "scalping knife." The sheath is of buckskin, beautifully decorated with sewn porcupine quillwork. (Courtesy John Painter Collection, Cincinnati)

Right: *An early print shows colonists watching Mohegan(?) warriors performing a "Dance Preparatory to War." The so-called King Philip's War of the 1670s, in which English colonists tried to break the power of a loose confederation of tribes—the Pequots, Narragansetts and Wampanoags, led by Metacom (known as "King Philip"), caused great devastation on both sides. In proportion to the population, the "short, vicious war inflicted greater casualties than any other war in American history." (Lepore, 1998:xi)*

Below: *Boy's Chippewa soft-soled moccasins. Stealth of movement was a skill of great importance. (Taylor Collection, Hastings, U.K.)*

is clearly indicated by the observations of Samuel de Champlain who, in 1609, reported that Huron and Northern Algonquian war leaders identified each individual with a special stick, a foot (0.3m) or so in length. Their leaders were given somewhat longer sticks and a square, of size up to 6 feet (1.8m.), was marked on the ground. The strategist then arranged the sticks according to his battle plan and briefed the members of the war-party on the order and rank to be observed when the engagement took place. Each individual noted their position and responsibilities. Rehearsals took place, the warriors randomly mixing and then reassembling, until the pattern was deemed sufficiently correct for competent battle.[2]

The use of light-weight, tough, soft-soled moccasins of deer or moosehide and bark canoes, ensured that movement of Woodland warriors could be silent and rapid whilst powdered, dried maize carried in buckskin bags, ensured a good supply of nutritious and easily prepared food. Weapons were the bow, stone and wooden-headed clubs and, on occasions, a spear and armor. All these combined to produce a formidable Woodland warrior of marked efficiency and skill.[3]

Use of trees for cover, separation from their fellow warriors, stealth to ambush and cover of darkness or storm, were techniques well developed in the Woodlands. Such tactics showed skillful and intelligent use of the environment so that intertribal battles resulted in little loss of life.

A major characteristic of aboriginal-type warfare in the Woodlands, was the individual freedom of action that warriors had in comparison to the more disciplined European soldiers. Nevertheless, as has been discussed, tactical plans were formulated by experienced war leaders, together with much pre-war ritual which evoked the higher powers. Special war regalia and body painting was adopted together with personal protective amulets which instilled confidence and courage. One early observer described a common form of headdress as "in the fashion of a cock's comb." (Gookin in Malone, 1991:20) This was of deer and porcupine hair with turkey as well as eagle feathers. The cock turkey was well known for its bravery in fighting and it has been recorded that warriors in battle not infrequently imitated its gobble.[4]

Below: *The forested areas of New England, home of the Pennacook, Pocumtuck, Mohegan, Pequot, Narragansett and Wampanoag. Several of these tribes formed a loose alliance and in the 1670s attempted to wipe out English colonists. Warfare in such heavily wooded areas favored combat at short range; in both warfare and the hunt, the ability to strike a fatal wound with the first arrow was considered to be a vital skill.*

Above: *An Eastern Sioux chief, Iron Bull, wearing an unusual headdress. It is made of the entire headskin of a wapiti or deer, complete with horns, the eyes being defined with large brass buttons. Such headgear could be employed as a disguise, so enabling a hunter to get close to his quarry. This man's ability, bravery and skill as a hunter is stated by his impressive necklace of the claws of a grizzly bear.*

Contrasting tactics: the Pequot and the English

The nature of, and tactics employed by, the Woodland tribes in warfare, became increasingly apparent in the seventeenth century by two major conflicts which occurred in this period. First, the Pequot War in the vicinity of present-day Connecticut (1636–1637) and later, the so-called King Philip's War of 1675–1676, which involved most of southern New England.

The Pequot—an abbreviation of Paquatauog, meaning "destroyers"—were a powerful Algonquian Connecticut tribe, whose territory extended down to Rhode Island. In 1636 they killed a white trader of questionable honesty; this, and subsequent acts of hostility, led to open warfare with the English colonists. Uniting with the Narragansett, Niantic and Mohegan, the colonists now marched against the Pequot killing some six hundred men, women and children. Those who survived, were forced into slavery or adopted by the surrounding tribes and they were strictly forbidden to refer to themselves as Pequots.

An uneasy peace prevailed for nearly forty years—but then came the so-called King Philip's War of 1675. Here, English colonists in the area of present-day southern New England, clashed with the surrounding Algonquians who were beginning to form a loose confederation to oppose further incursions by the colonists, into their homelands.

Foremost in these conflicts, were the Wampanoags, who resided less than sixty miles from the fast-growing Plymouth colony to the east. Led by the great sachem, Metacom (known to the whites as King Philip), the war escalated from the region of Narragansett Bay and extended north to the Nipmucks and Pocumtucks (in present-day Massachusetts) and west to the Connecticut River Valley—land of the Pequots and Mohegans. Within the space of a few months, an area covering more than 20,000 square miles became a dangerous field of war. The various tribes attacked and destroyed English towns and farms and colonial armies attempted to annihilate Indians in the various settlements throughout the region. It was a brutal clash of cultures and the starkly different strategies of war practiced by each side, became increasingly apparent. There were several factors, however, that were common to both. The pent up emotions led to little restraint on either side, with the brutal killing of women and children, horrendous torture and ghastly mutilation of the dead.

Death of Metacom

Metacom, for example, was shot down (12 August, 1676) in a swamp near present-day Mount Hope. In charge of the body was a certain Captain Benjamin Church, who announced that since Metacom "had caused many an Englishman's body to be unburied, and to rot above ground, not one of his bones should be buried." (Lepore, 1998:173) He now ordered that Metacom be beheaded and his body quartered. The quarters were hung in four trees and one hand was given to the Indian who shot him. Metacom's head was taken to Plymouth and there displayed on a tall post for public viewing.[5] Even when the war was over, tensions still remained "for decades." (ibid.) The legitimacy of the occupation of Indian lands, together with their savage conduct, caused deep concerns within the communities. As one recent historian has observed, the colonists would "never succeed at reconstructing themselves as 'true Englishmen.'" (ibid:175)

The ambuscade

A feature of American Indian warfare, was that conflict seldom incurred heavy losses.[6] The majority of tribes were too small to bear large losses without a danger to their survival. Land and game abundance, on the whole, eliminated sustained wars of conquest. Thus, compared with European, Indian warfare was markedly less destructive and when Indians, fighting alongside whites, observed the slaughter which was a feature of European warfare, many were genuinely appalled. The Narragansett, who sided with the English in the Pequot war of 1636–1637, refused to participate in acts "they found unacceptable to their notions of just conduct."

Below: *The death of Metacom, the Wampanoag chief, near present-day Mount Hope in August 1676. This ended "King Philip's War", which began after English colonists progressively expanded their territory much to the alarm of the indigenous population. Metacom's head was taken to Plymouth and publicly displayed. Such barbaric behavior raised the question as to whether the colonists would ever be true Englishmen. (see text)*

Left: *Valuable trade knives were generally carried in elaborate sheaths, as shown here. This is identified as from the Red River Cree and dating from c.1820. The upper section is embellished with loom quillwork, which is typical of Cree material produced at this time. It has an inner lining of birch bark, which encloses the metal blade. Its symmetrical shape would suggest that it was worn at the neck, rather than on the belt. (Courtesy John Painter Collection, Cincinnati)*

Opposite page: *A Chippewa knife sheath decorated with loom beadwork and said to date from the mid-nineteenth century. It has a birch bark liner and the fringes are embellished with ovoid beads, together with blue and red yarn tassels. (Courtesy John Painter Collection, Cincinnati)*

(ibid:116) In this Pequot War—where in one encounter the English burned hundreds of women and children who were trapped in a compound—the Narragansett pulled back from the slaughter, crying "*Mach it, mach it*; that is, It is naught, it is naught, because it is too furious, and slays too many men." (Underhill In ibid:116) Rather than open ground conflict, the Woodland Indians' favored form of offensive warfare, was the **ambush**. It was a technique common also to hunting practices, where the animal was lured into a trap by calls or bait. Careful selection of the location where the surrounding terrain ensured good concealment for the war-party, was the first consideration. This ideally, was combined with natural barriers— rivers, lakes, cliffs, heavy foliage—which prevented escape and maximized the effectiveness of the surprise. When the Narragansett discussed with the English the best mode of raiding an unfortified camp of Pequot, they suggested just such tactics: "That the assault would be in the night, when they are commonly more secure and at home,...[when they could enter] and do what execution they please...Before the assault be given, an ambush be laid behind them between them and the swamp, to prevent their flight, etc." (Winthrop In Malone, 1991:22)

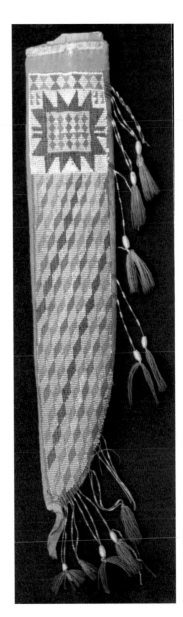

The seventeenth century colonists largely looked upon such war-fare as devious—"skulking" they said. As one authority has related of the colonists' attitude, "They wanted the Indians to fight in the open, but with more discipline and with greater willingness to suffer and inflict grievous losses." (Malone, 1991:23) The fact that the Woodland tribes did not fight in precise formations or "hold their ground with the tenacity that the English expected of soldiers" puzzled the colonists. (ibid.) What they largely failed to grasp was that such warfare was carried out with considerable skill, both in planning and its execution.[7]

Given the nature of the terrain and the indigenous weaponry available, these aboriginal military tactics were generally highly efficient. Towards the middle of the seventeenth century, however, the situation markedly changed. Now firearms, particularly the flintlock, were increasingly adopted by the Woodland tribes. The acute eyesight and sharp reflexes of the Indian warrior ensured that they rapidly became highly proficient in the use of guns; in turn, warfare tactics

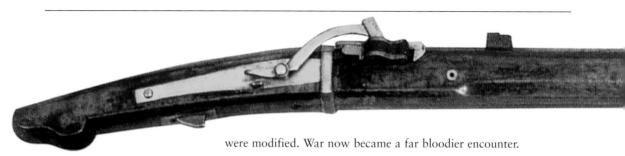

were modified. War now became a far bloodier encounter.

Above: *Matchlock muskets were introduced from Europe by colonists in the early 1600s. Initially desired by Indians, their limitations were soon apparent. The firing mechanism was slow and it required the use of a rest, so it was ineffective in Indian-style warfare. When the flintlock was adopted in the 1650s, Indians modified their tactics and blended the best of aboriginal and European warfare to great success.*

War trophies

Much intertribal warfare in the eastern part of North America, centred around the capture of females as spoils of war. Not only did they help maintain the tribal population but they were invaluable as burden carriers—often being traded to other tribes and used virtually as slaves. Thus, Father Marquette, who visited the Illinois in 1673, observed that this tribe "make themselves dreaded by the Distant tribes... whither they go to procure Slaves; these they barter, selling them at a high price to other Nations, in exchange for other Wares." (Kenton, 1956:351)

"Slaves to the Victor"

When scalps were taken, they were actually viewed more than simply a trophy of war.

A widespread concept was that the scalps represented those of the enemy whose souls would be slaves to the victor in the next world. Scalping was, thus, an insurance for the good life hereafter. Marquette (1673) reported that amongst the "Nations of Louisiana," the war chiefs bestowed names upon warriors according to their conduct in battle. "To deserve the title of a great man-slayer, it is necessary to have taken 10 slaves or to have carried off 20 scalps." (ibid:417)

One early observer commented on the skill displayed in the removal of the scalp: "They remove it as nicely as one would the skin of a rabbit." (Nadeau, 1938:180) The skin was cut to the bone, starting at the front, in the middle of the forehead. It was then followed around and behind one ear, then in the back of the neck and around the other ear. The edge of the skin was then carefully raised so that the victor could "peel off the scalp as easily as one would a glove from the hand!" (ibid:182) The custom of removing other body parts

as trophies—hairy parts of the skin or other pieces—received greater impetus, by the bounty system. It was sometimes taken to extremes. A Virginian Indian was completely skinned and "from it were made a saddle, ball bags, and belts." (Friederici, 1907:436)[8]

Tears of grief: scalp identification

Such scalps were not infrequently stretched on hoops and ingeniously identified by use of motifs and symbols which indicated the location and circumstances under which they were taken. A little reported episode (1782), makes reference to more than a thousand scalps taken by the Iroquois and, through their agent, sent to Frederick Haldimand, then Governor of Canada. These were to indicate the activities and the continued loyalty of the Seneca to the British against the breakaway colonies during the period of the American Revolution. Forty-three of the scalps were of Congress soldiers who had been killed in different skirmishes with the Seneca. The scalps were stretched on black hoops, some 4 inches (10cm) in diameter and the inside of the skin was painted red; each had a small black dot to indicate that they had been killed by bullets.

Sixty-two scalps were of white farmers; the hoops were painted red, the skin painted brown, and marked with a hoe surrounded by a dark circle to denote that they had been surprised in the night. Adjacent was a painted motif of a war hatchet to indicate that they had been killed by that weapon. Almost a hundred scalps were

Below: Grasping the scalp-lock. Early observers in Eastern North America noted that warriors were named in accordance with conduct in battle. To deserve the title of "great man-slayer," he would have taken some twenty scalps.

stretched on hoops painted green, to show that they had been killed in the fields. A large white circle with a dot for the sun, identified that the incidents took place during the day. There were bullet motifs on some, hatchets on others. Most sinister, were eighteen scalps marked with a yellow flame "to denote their being of prisoners burned alive after being scalped, [and tortured]." One of these was identified as an American clergyman, his "dog collar" being fixed "to the hoop of his scalp." (Eckert, 1992:285)

There are further graphic details, such as the hair braided to show that the victims were mothers. Hoops painted blue and the skin of the scalp painted yellow upon which were painted small tadpole-like figures represented "tears of grief" of their relations. (ibid.)

Such was the importance of the scalp to state the actions and proficiency of the individual in warfare. Other methods, face and body marking and certain types of dress and headgear were also employed to illustrate success on the warpath.

Bounties for scalps

Scalping was given a major impetus when, in the 1630s, the Puritans of New England began offering bounty payments for the **heads** of

Above: A very fine knife and sheath from the region of the Great Lakes, probably dating from about 1780. The sharp-pointed steel blade of the knife would suggest its effectiveness for scalping. Such narrow blades could be relatively easily inserted through an incision between skull and scalp. As one scholar has observed, the scalp could then be peeled off "as easily as one would a glove from the hand." (See p.33) This knife has a horn handle with a finely carved turtle in raised relief on the top (possibly a reference to clan affiliation?) The sheath is of black buckskin embellished with porcupine quills and moosehair. It was probably worn at the neck. (Courtesy John Painter Collection, Cincinnati)

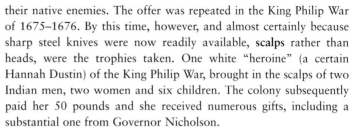

Below: *A scalp stretched on a hoop, which has been decorated with porcupine quills and split cane. This is obviously an early specimen, and it is very similar to those sent to Frederick Haldimand (Governor of Canada) by the Seneca in the 1780s, to demonstrate their loyalty to the British. Many such scalps were painted with various motifs, which made reference to who the victims were and the manner in which they had been killed. (see pp.33–34)*

their native enemies. The offer was repeated in the King Philip War of 1675–1676. By this time, however, and almost certainly because sharp steel knives were now readily available, **scalps** rather than heads, were the trophies taken. One white "heroine" (a certain Hannah Dustin) of the King Philip War, brought in the scalps of two Indian men, two women and six children. The colony subsequently paid her 50 pounds and she received numerous gifts, including a substantial one from Governor Nicholson.

A decade or so later, in 1688, the French Canadian authorities were prepared to pay ten beaver skins for every scalp of their enemies —white or Indian. This was a high price, being equivalent in Montreal to the price of a flintlock gun together with four pounds of gunpowder and forty pounds of lead shot.

In later wars, in which white colonists were involved, bounties for scalps increased in value, inciting the practice to greater intensity and it now became a profitable activity. As one scholar observed, "The alluring profits and the growing difficulty of securing the trophy led some to skillfully make two or even more scalps out of one, and to other, more grave, abuses; members of friendly tribes and even the white countrymen of the scalpers were not safe, and even graves were made to yield victims." (Friederici, 1907:434)

This was a far cry from the earlier, more honorable custom of scalp-taking, when such trophies were a visible proof of personal bravery. A type of "medal" acquired—often with considerable tactical skill—on the field of war.

Fortified villages of the Iroquois

Early descriptions of Iroquois villages, refer to elaborate fortifications consisting of a stockade and sometimes a moat. They were constructed by driving two rows of tree trunks into the ground, inclining each pair so that they crossed some 16.5 feet (5m.) from the ground, the space between being filled with logs. The trunks were carefully bound together at

Below: *This early print depicts a battle between Iroquois and a mixed force of Huron, Montagnais and Ottawa. The latter are led by French explorer Samuel de Champlain, supported by other arquebus-armed soldiers. The palm trees, hammocks and nakedness are probably artist's inventions. The formation shows Champlain's influence; European military tactics favored moving forward en masse, firing toward the enemy. Indian warfare favored scattered, silently-moving individuals who maximized the use of trees and rocks for protection. In European combat, because little effort was made to aim at anyone, officers were safe as the soldiers in formation. This changed when Indians acquired the musket and, with skillful use, killed the leaders first.*

their point of crossing and horizontal beams were laid into the Vs, forming a narrow walkway protected on the outer side with bark slabs. Notched poles on the inner part of the palisade were used as "rough ladders," giving the defenders access to the protected walkway. (Bishop, 1949:232)

They were formidable forts, designed and erected with considerable skill and group coordination. When, in 1615, one such village was attacked by the Huron (supported by gun-armed French under Champlain), they were, to their consternation, unable to succeed in getting the Onondaga inhabitants to surrender.

Other than the supporting French, the raid on the Onondaga village was typical of one mode of intertribal warfare between Iroquoian speaking tribes. Indeed, such was the nature of the Iroquoian warfare pattern, it is unlikely that the Huron would have actually considered the Onondaga siege a failure, because hostile encounters were not generally a struggle for hunting territory or land, but a test of a warrior's bravery to take a scalp or two and, perhaps, prisoners for torture and on this occasion, they succeeded in doing just that.

Whites joining Indian war-parties, not infrequently encountered more than they bargained for. Such was the case of the Dutch commander who, in 1626, joined the Mohegan to invade the Mohawk. When only several miles distant from Fort Orange (the site of present-day Albany), they were confronted by a party of Mohawks. Although the Mohawk were only armed with bows and arrows, they were employed with great skill against the gun-armed Dutch. In the ensuing battle, the Dutch commander and three of his men were killed. A "postscript warning" filtered back to Fort Orange, clearly replete in grim humor: one of the Dutch (probably the commander) was cooked and eaten by the victorious Mohawks![9]

Origin of Iroquoian war ethic

Prior to an expedition against the enemy and agreement having been reached in council, the Huron traditionally had a war feast which was prepared by the women. The origin of the feast—and it also went some way to explain the war-like nature of the Iroquois—was attributed in their mythology to a giant whom a number of Huron had encountered on the shore of a large lake. When failing to reply politely to his greeting, one of the Huron wounded the giant in its forehead. In punishment, the giant sowed the seeds of discord

Above: *Spun and braided buffalo-hair prisoner ties, wrapped at intervals with pericardium, red-dyed horsehair and porcupine quills, Sauk and Fox (?), c.1800. Constraints of this type symbolized a subservient enemy; attached rattles betrayed him if he tried to escape. (Courtesy John Painter Collection, Cincinnati)*

amongst the Huron, but before he disappeared into the earth, he recommended the war and *Ononharoia* feasts and the use of the war cry, *wiiiiii*. The feast was accompanied by singing and dancing by the young warriors who uttered abuse against the enemy with promises of victory and as they moved from one end of the longhouse to the other, "under the pretext of doing it in jest, [they] would knock down others whom they did not like." (Trigger, 1969:46)

The sport of war

It was not unusual for several hundred Huron warriors to lay siege to an Iroquois village, generally the Seneca who lived closest to Huron territory. Such expeditions usually took place in the summer, when there was plenty of leaf cover and often had an air of an outing, as Champlain commented on the prelude to one Huron-Iroquois battle: "This war had much of the character of an organized sport." (Bishop, 1949:147)[10] The men travelled slowly towards enemy country, fishing and hunting along the way. On crossing Lake Ontario by canoe to the south shore, they would then hide, split up into smaller groups and then travel on foot to the Iroquois villages. Women and children were not infrequently captured before the village itself was put to siege. The principal weapon used in pre-or early contact times, both by the Iroquois and the Huron, was the stone-headed or wooden ballheaded club. The latter was a formidable weapon at close range; commonly made of ironwood and up to 2 feet (60cm) in length, it had a large knob or ball at the head, some 4.5 to 10 inches (12–15 cm) in diameter, which was often carved with animal figures, perhaps emblematic of the owner's personal totem and protective power. As has been discussed elsewhere, the ballheaded club was later superseded by the trade metal pipe tomahawk and, likewise, the bow and arrow replaced by the gun, the latter having a particular impact on warfare tactics—for example, the abandonment of wooden body armor and change in battle formation.

Carrying the casualties

In all cases, casualties were usually few in number, the young aspiring warriors laying emphasis on performing acts of daring. Generally, after a few injuries and deaths, the attackers withdrew to their

Above: *Pickaxe-type tomahawk, dating from at least 1725. This may have been a relatively common form of tomahawk, as used by such tribes as the Delaware and Susquehannock. The blade is a celt of greenish stone about 12 inches (30cm) in length, attached to a 20-inch (50cm) wooden handle, which is decorated with flat pieces of wampum stuck on the surface. This specimen may have been acquired by Swedish settlers who had a colony on the Lower Delaware River. It is now in the National Museum, Copenhagen, Hb.26. (Sketch by Ted Brasser)*

Below: *A Mohawk warrior as he would have appeared c.1750. This careful reconstruction is based on detailed research by anthropologist W.C. Sturtevant of the Smithsonian Institution, Washington. Tight-fitting leggings and soft-soled moccasins ensured stealth in the hunt and on the warpath.*

temporary forts which they commonly built near the enemy village. Pitched battles tended to be avoided and if reinforcements from other settlements were imminent, the attackers left for home. The wounded were carried home in a makeshift basket sling on the backs of their companions and, whilst it was a practical means of transport through the heavily wooded forest, it was appallingly uncomfortable for the injured. Champlain, who was himself wounded in the leg and knee by two Iroquois arrows, describes how the Huron men fabricated the frame of hickory or elm, attaching a seat with straps of hide or of the plaited inner bark of elm. The frame and burden were supported by a tumpline across the carrier's forehead and the wounded warrior sat on the seat, his legs under his chin and tightly bound in position. Champlain described his ordeal—undoubtedly an extremely unpleasant one experienced by many an immobilized Iroquoian warrior: "It was impossible to move any more than a little child in its swaddling clothes... and this causes the wounded great and extreme pain. I can say this indeed from my own case, having been carried for several days because I was unable to stand, chiefly on account of the arrow-wound I had received in my knee, for never did I find myself in such a hell as during this time: for the pain I suffered from the wound in my knee was nothing in comparison with what I endured tied and bound on the back of one of our savages." (ibid:238)

39

Such journeys clearly subjected the helpless incumbent to endless tossing, buffeting and whipping by the tree branches and half, sometimes complete, immersion in water. All this, as the bearer made his way through forest and streams, but it was greatly preferable to falling into the hands of Iroquois enemies!

The savagery of the Iroquois-Huron War (1648–1650)

Early explorers found much to admire in Iroquoian society; they describe, for example, the superb physique of the men and the beauty of the young women. There was surprisingly little internal conflict within the crowded villages and all were fond of laughter and jokes, applied good sense and justice in their affairs, showed great hospitality and, at times, great kindness. They had an acuteness of sense, great courage, endurance and were stoic to pain.

The treatment of prisoners, however, was another matter and the horrendous tortures stunned and appalled white observers. Such ritual torture was part of Huron and Iroquois psychology and it was far less practiced by the neighboring Algonquian-speaking tribes.

Capture of enemies was an honorable war deed which all aspiring warriors attempted to achieve. The importance of such deeds was well recognized by both captors and captives. Thus, on occasions, if several men claimed the capture of a particular prisoner, the prisoner himself would be requested to designate his official captor. In so doing, wily captured Iroquoians, who were well versed in the psychology of intertribal warfare, not infrequently named another who was less involved in his capture. This could strike a note of discord amongst his captors and sometimes, rather than allow the honor to go to the wrong man, he was helped to escape.

The Master of War

It is clear that religious concepts were at the basis of much of this ritual cruelty. Thus, the Jesuit priest, Father Isaac Jogues recorded that these tortures were actually a sacrifice to the Mohawk's God of War, *Aireskoi*. One unfortunate captive woman was systematically burned "all over her body…at every burn which they caused, by applying lighted torches," a sage exclaimed in a loud voice, "Aireskoi we offer [you] this victim, whom we burn for [you], that [you]

Above: *Ritual cruelty was practiced in intertribal warfare, it being early recorded by white observers. The custom was particularly well-developed by the Iroquois and Huron. It seemed to reflect some unusual psychology of the Iroquoian people and was far less employed by their Algonquian neighbors. Such tortures were said to be a sacrifice to Gods of War, such as the Mohawk's* Aireskoi. *The slow torture was considered by the Iroquois to be a mark of respect to an enemy's bravery and fortitude. This illustration appeared in the memoirs of the seventeenth-century Dutch traveler, David de Vries.*

mayest be filled with her flesh and render us ever anew victorious over our enemies." (Hewitt, Hodge ed., 1909:923) The woman's body was subsequently cut up and sent to various villages for ritual cannibalism—all to salute the "Master... of War." (ibid.)

Saouandanancous' ordeal

The historian, Francis Parkman, has described in great detail the fate of one Iroquois prisoner who was captured by the Huron during the savage Iroquois-Huron War of 1648–1650.[11] *Saouandanancous* was brought in by his Huron captors and adopted by an elderly chief who, having lost a son, had hoped that *Saouandanancous* might take his place; the prisoner's hands, however, had been seriously injured, and because of this—whilst treating him with courtesy and an outward show of genuine affection—he was condemned to die. He was put to death by fire so **carefully** and **skillfully** applied, that it took him over twelve hours to die. Astoundingly, his tormentors

Below: *"William Penn's Treaty with the Indians," an engraving after the original painting by Benjamin West (1771). Penn founded the colony in 1682, naming the area Pennsylvania in his father's honor. In 1683, he made his "Great Treaty" with local Indians—Iroquoian and Algonquian —which, according to Voltaire, was "the only treaty not sworn to and never broken." Penn recognized the importance of gift-giving as a crucial factor in negotiations with Indian people. Several accoutrements shown here are now in the British Museum, London. (King, 1991:34-47)*

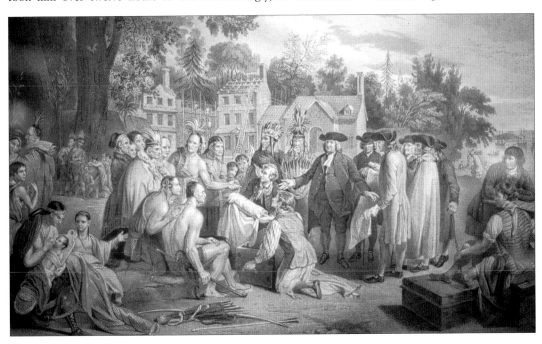

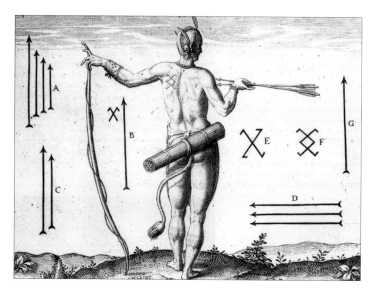

Above: *Warfare was a passion of Woodland tribes. Tactics differed significantly from the Europeans and goals were generally different. Battle after sunset was unusual; being first to kill an enemy was more important than how many killed. Symbolic military insignia, however, was common to both—tattoos, headgear and body paint were equivalent to medals, braiding and epaulettes. Here, C & D refer to important individuals from Secoton village, E, F & G were symbols used by Pomeioc war chiefs and A identifies the Roanoke chief,* Wingino. *This engraving is based on a sixteenth-century painting by English artist John White.*

showed no signs of lack of self control and as each applied his particular torture, they spoke to the prisoner in a kindly way. Equally extraordinary, is that *Saouandanancous* demonstrated the courage and endurance expected of an Iroquois warrior. During intervals between the torture he not only reported on Hurons who had been adopted into his tribe, but sang as well. When he finally expired, he was cut up and small pieces of his flesh distributed for eating.

In 1609, Champlain told of a similar episode; after the battle at Ticonderoga, one of the dozen or so prisoners was selected for torture. The Huron harangued him with the cruelties which he and members of his tribe had practiced on them and that he should prepare himself to experience as much. They told him to sing "if he had the heart" and Champlain reports that he did "but it was a very sad song to hear." (Bishop, 1949:150)

Weaponry: "Most desperate marksman"—the bow

Prior to the introduction of firearms, the bow was the most effective weapon for killing at a distance. It was the foremost Native American weapon first observed and described in some detail, by white colonists in the New England area.

A precursor of the bow in North America, was the atlatl or spear thrower, which could be used with deadly effect in open terrain. The atlatl was widely distributed in North America, being used from the Arctic to the Southwest. (Taylor, 2001:10, 59-62, 80) It did not, however, gain favor in the dense woodland country of North America. Here, the spear seems to have been employed in a symbolic context—to denote rank, it being carried by the "captains" and not by the common warrior. (Wood In Malone, 1991:19)

There is little question that the Woodland bow lacked the power of the traditional English long bow. The Indian bow had a "pull" not exceeding 50lbs. (approx. 23 kg.) at full draw, whilst the English long bow could exceed 70lbs. (approx. 34 kg.) For this reason, Indian bows were initially dismissed by the colonists as being too weak to render significant damage.

Subsequent events, however, demonstrated that it could have deadly effect when at close range and in the hands of a skilled warrior. In 1636, when the Pequot killed several of Lion Gardiner's men at Fort Saybrook, Gardiner reported that "the body of one man shot through, the arrow going in at the right side, the head sticking fast, half through a rib on the left side." He sent both the arrow and the man's rib to officials in Massachusetts Bay Colony, "because they had said the arrows of the Indians were of no force." (Malone, 1991:15)[12]

By stealth, the Woodland Indian generally attempted to get as near to his quarry as possible before shooting. At close range, the arrow moved rapidly and virtually in a straight line towards the intended victim, giving man or animal little time to react. The technique was highly successful in both war and hunt; it was a skill acquired in childhood, Indian boys being encouraged to practice with the bow and arrow on a daily basis. Other skills with the bow, greatly impressed the colonists, such as the warriors' ability to hit small rapidly moving targets and to fire in quick succession. In the latter case, for example, it is reliably reported that efficient warriors could dextrously shoot up to ten arrows before a musket could be reloaded. Little wonder that Indians made only limited use of the cumbersome matchlock musket; not until the 1660s when the flintlock became readily available, did the gun replace the bow.[13]

Below: Thayendanegea, *or Joseph Brant, war chief of the Six Nations. A painting by George Catlin, based on an earlier portrait by E. Ames (c.1780). A biographer described Thayendanegea as having an "air and mien of one born to command." (Stone, 1864). He sided with the British in 1776, maintaining a staunch friendship for the English throughout his life.*

"Unerring and deadly aim:" the tomahawk

The tomahawk was second only to the bow as a favored weapon. It came in a variety of forms but an early, commonly used type, was made entirely of wood with a long handle and a heavy round head. On occasions, a flint or bone point was inserted into the ball, making it a particularly dangerous weapon at close quarters. Early reports make reference to the **throwing** of the tomahawk, such that it struck the skull or back of the pursued. The thrower had to know how many times the tomahawk would rotate in flight over a given distance and obviously be able to estimate the range between himself and the enemy—both accurately and quickly. As one authority commented, "Should he miss, he would be disarmed and then might find himself the hunted, instead of the armed hunter." (Peterson, 1971:15) It has been suggested that such skill and accuracy was acquired through the custom of throwing at small trees as a camp pastime. Utmost dexterity, unerring and deadly aim, an art of directing and regulating its motion, are the various descriptions in the early literature which relate to the efficient use of the tomahawk in Woodland Indian warfare.[14]

Tomahawk metaphors

The importance and constant use of the tomahawk as a weapon, caused it to be identified as both a symbol for war and for war potential. It was employed as a metaphor in speeches and ceremonials when war was discussed or when peace was being concluded. Actual tomahawks or renderings of them on wampum belts were sent to other tribes. Thus, when peace was made after the

Below: *A Chippewa war-honor badge. This was worn on the right arm of Odjib'we, a distinguished warrior of the Mississippi band of the Chippewa in Minnesota. Made of skunk skin, it signified that he had once caught a wounded Sioux by the arm. The left illustration shows the front of the badge and the right the back.*

Above: *A Harper's Ferry (Model 1803) flintlock rifle 0.54 caliber. Prior to the introduction of the flintlock was the arquebus (see p.46). Although at times displaying frightening killing power, it was ineffective in the Woodland environment. The flintlock, on the other hand—which was available to such tribes as the Mohawk as early as 1650—was rapidly adopted by Indians. Their ready comprehension generally made them superior in its use to the average colonist.*

Below: *Iroquois beaded "Glengarry" hat, c.1860. A direct adaptation of military Highlanders' headgear, it came to be distinctively Iroquois. (Taylor Collection, Hastings, U.K.)*

defeat of the Algonquians by the Iroquois (1670), a council was held. At this time "six tomahawks were buried—one for each of the Five Nations, and one representing the defeated tribe." (ibid:16) The Algonquian weapon was buried first and the others placed on top of it. In the event of hostilities being resumed, "the Algonquian warriors would have to raise the weapons of their foes from their own, and thus be reminded of their defeat." (ibid.)

Phrases were developed at this time, using the tomahawk as a metaphor for war. Thus, a belligerent statement was referred to as a "tomahawk speech" and to "'take up the hatchet' was to declare war." (ibid.)[15]

Skinning and scalping: the knife

Knives of stone, bone, wood and sometimes copper, were used by Indians for aeons. Although considered an invaluable accessory, it was not commonly employed in war.

When Captain John Smith first wrote of the Virginia Indians in 1612, he observed the importance of the knife in the Indians' life: "For his knife he hath the splinter of a reed to cut his feathers in forme. With this knife also, he will joint a Deare or any beast, shape his shooes, buskins, mantels... To make the nock of his arrow hee hath the tooth of a Bever set in a sticke, wherewith he grateth it by degrees." (Smith In Peterson, 1957:116)

One of the things Indians wanted most in their initial contacts with Europeans, was the steel knife. These had a profound effect on their lifestyle, enabling previous virtually impossible tasks to now be achieved with great ease. As has been observed, "the knife had been an indispensable tool before. It became more so now. And it became a favorite weapon." (Peterson, 1957:117)

Some of the best knives had fine bone handles which were inlaid with horn or bone. Knives for scalping are listed in a number of trade goods accounts. Although there is some question as to the validity of the term "scalping knife," it does seem that a certain style was produced to increase the efficiency of the scalping process. Such designs had a narrow blade which could be relatively easily worked up between the scalp and the skull, after the initial incision had been made.

Arquebus to flintlock: the impact of the gun

There is little doubt that the early style of muzzle-loading, smooth-bore, first used by the early explorers in eastern North America, initially enjoyed respect in the minds of the Indians. A dramatic demonstration of the awesome power of the arquebus occurred when, in 1609, the French explorer Samuel de Champlain, killed two Iroquois chiefs and wounded another with a single blast. These chiefs were leading a party of almost two hundred Iroquois warriors—probably Mohawk—but the frightening power of the arquebus caused them to fall back in dismay. The armor which several of them wore, was no protection against lead musket balls—although it had served them well for aeons against arrows.

The gun was at first likened in the minds of the Indians, to be power of the thunder or lightning. Crippling or killing game or an enemy at a distance, by hurling a tiny missile so swiftly that the eye could not follow its flight, "filled the primitive Indian with wonder and admiration." (Ewers, 1968:34) It was, however, out of all proportion to its actual effectiveness, particularly as a fighting weapon in Indian warfare.

The early musket relied on the so-called matchlock mechanism, where a specially treated cord was lit prior to firing. The process was slow and fraught with hazards—wet weather, the glow, odor and, of course, the actual production, as well as the limited efficiency, of the

Above: *Ojibwa warrior "The Ottaway," a painting by George Catlin, c.1835. Face painting and head feathers clearly make reference to warpath exploits, although, unlike the war-honor badge on p.44, the meaning is not recorded.*

Below: Odjib'we's *war-honor feathers (Chippewa). His prowess in war won him the right to wear specially-decorated and cut eagle feathers. Each of them referred to him taking a Sioux scalp. Three of the feathers are notched; the right to wear these was acquired by both killing and scalping Sioux. The un-notched feathers referred to those killed by others—but who he scalped. The dots of white fur indicate the number of bullets in his gun at the time of securing the scalp. Odjib'we explained that four feathers could be counted for the death of each Sioux; one was "worn by the man who killed him, one by the man who scalped him, and the others by men who assisted in the scalping." (Densmore, 1913:62)*

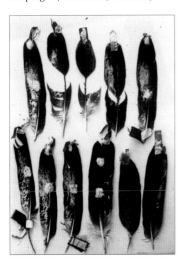

cord itself. In addition, the arquebus weighed close to 20lbs. (approx. 9kg.) and needed a forked rest to support it when firing.

Such weaponry—used on **both** sides in the European wars and by musketeers in close formation—was relatively ineffective when confronting Indians in the forests of eastern North America. As has been recorded, "[they] faced Indian warriors with a long tradition of success through stealth and surprise. Indians used the forest as an ally against their enemies... A warrior who suddenly darted from the brush was no easy target..." (Malone, 1991:32-33)

By the mid-1650s, however, the more effective flintlock musket was increasingly adopted. Here, a flint strikes a frizzen or battery producing sparks which ignite the priming powder and relatively rapid firing was possible. The limitations imposed on the arquebus, were now largely eliminated. These advantages were quickly recognized by Indians who saw that such a weapon more clearly matched their style of military and hunting tactics.

The most proficient at this time in the use of the musket, were the Mohawk who were amongst the first to procure them from the Dutch. They quickly subjugated the Lenni Lenape (Delaware) confederation and then initiated a campaign of conquest. Their war-parties traveled as far as the Mississippi in the west and shores of the Hudson Bay to the north.[16]

Largely supplied to facilitate hunting efficiency in the fur trade, guns became increasingly available and by the 1670s, most of the tribes east of the Great Lakes, were armed with the new weapon. In both war and the hunt, they became adept in its use—generally superior marksmen in comparison to the average colonist. A move away from over-dependence on the white man's expertise was also developed. Indians became proficient in the repair of their own weapons and casting their own shot. They also re-sharpened worn or broken gunflints. The skill was widely distributed: a Narragansett site on Rhode Island revealed an Indian blacksmith kit and over four hundred flintlock parts were found in a single Iroquois grave which "must have belonged to a very capable and busy repairman." (ibid:72)

Virtually, the only skill that the Woodland Indians then lacked, it seems, was the making of gunpowder—although there is evidence that they tried very hard to acquire the knowledge!

CHAPTER III

Ikatsita

("Going to war" - Western Apache)

Apache War Ethos
& Tactics

*"The Apaches... danced for seven hours
to get a better oracle.. .but the captain must soon die"*
(Bourke, c. 1875).

Below: *Apache warrior Army scouts, at Camp Apache in c.1871. They show two physical types: strong chiseled features or heavier features maybe from Spanish/Mexican blood.*

THE APACHE were linguistically affiliated with the Athapaskan-speaking people of the far north. Generally referred to as the Southern Athapaskans, they left the Canadian Subarctic region about 1500 AD and migrated south. They finally settled in the area of what is now New Mexico, Arizona and the Mexican states of Sonora and

Chihauhau. This roughly coincided with the arrival of the Spanish, who by 1600 were colonizing the Rio Grande valley and forming alliances with some of the Pueblo tribes who, for thousands of years, had occupied the region.

Raiding was a vital component of Apache economy and culture and the relative richness of the Spanish and Indian settlements in horses and cattle made attractive targets. The settlements, thus, became an important resource to the Apache economy and lifeway, such that "By 1700 the Spaniards and their Indian allies were locked in [constant] warfare with the Athapaskans." (Porter 1986:6)

The Southern Athapaskans consisted of seven distinct tribal groups the largest being the Navajo followed by the Western Apache. Others were the Jicarilla, Lipan, Mescalero, Chiricahua and Kiowa-Apache. The Western Apache were in turn divided into five subtribes —the San Carlos, Cibecue, White Mountain and the Northern and Southern Tonto.

Although the Chiricahuas were a separate tribe, they were closely aligned with the Western Apaches both in culture and language. Of all the Apache tribes, it was perhaps the Chiricahuas who were best known to history. In the Apache wars of the 1880s, their leaders such as Cochise, Mangas Coloradas, Geronimo and Chato (to name a few) became well-known as the various Apache bands carried out guerilla-like warfare against Spanish, Mexicans and Americans alike.

Skilled fighters: the characteristics of an Apache warrior
One army officer—Captain John G. Bourke—who knew the Apache well, was greatly impressed by their warrior class. Many, he said, were tall and "straight as arrows." Their heads were long, with aquiline noses, chiseled lips and chins and "flashing eyes." They were very powerfully built, "straight, sinewy, well-muscled, extremely strong in the lower limbs, provided with a round barrel chest, showing good lung power, keen, intelligent-looking eyes, good head, and a mouth showing determination, decision, and cruelty." (Bourke, 1891: 123-124)[1]

The powers of endurance of the Apache warrior and the knowledge of the country, were admired by all who fought against them. One well-used war tactic was to exhaust the opposition by pursuit or planned retreat, then attack—but only when there was a

Below: Goyathlay, "One who yawns!", a Chiricahua Apache leader. Better known as Geronimo—probably one of the most famous names in Native American history—he fought both General Crook in 1882 and finally capitulated to General Miles in 1886. Geronimo was fiercely independent and uncompromising, maintaining his freedom and inheritance to the end. He died in February 1909.

Below: *An Apache warrior, or hunter, depicted as he may have appeared about 1880, by the artist Ernest Berke. Such individuals had incredible powers of endurance; when on a war or hunting party, they could travel for days by foot, little affected by the torrid heat of Apacheria. Essential were the rawhide-soled boot-moccasins, as shown here, for stealthy, fast movement. This ability led one army officer to describe pursuit of Apache as, "degenerat[ing] into a will-o'-th'-wisp chase." (see p.58)*

high chance of success. Retreat was considered prudent rather than stand ground and fight, particularly if it saved the life of a comrade.

Apache warriors could travel on foot for several days unaffected by the oft-high temperatures of the Apacheria terrain. They could cover up to one hundred miles in one day "usually losing the most determined pursuers." (Porter, 1986:7) Having acute vision, it was possible for them to discern movement and identify its nature for up to a distance of thirty miles.

Such endurance stemmed from the traditional Apache lifeway. Boys were given bows and arrows at a very early age and were encouraged to hunt birds and small animals and sham battles, foot races and use of lances ensured daily exercise of muscles and steadiness of aim. They were taught the names of the various desert animals and plants together with their attributes, knowledge essential for trapping and surviving in an oft-times hostile environment. This experience and training developed individuals who could maximize desert resources to the best effect; they could endure great suffering and fatigue and survive without both food and water for unusually long periods.

Such men, not unlike many of the animals which occupied Apacheria and elsewhere (see for example Chapter IV), were tough, resourceful and difficult to kill. A scalp now in a museum ethnographical collection has an accompanying note which vividly illustrates the immense tenacity of the Apache warrior. Returning on a raiding expedition to a Mexican settlement the leader was isolated from the main group by a party of some thirty Mexicans. The resulting encounter was graphically described: "The apache seems to have been a perfect devil to fight, he was leader of a party of eight, who had stolen and were driving home a herd of cattle when they were attacked by a party of about thirty mexicans, the owner of the scalp received three wounds, each of which would have been mortal, before he fell, and a mexican then went near him to give him a 'coup-de-grace' when he seized the mexicans lance, broke the staff, and killed his opponent, he was then shot at from a safe distance until he died and his scalp secured. With warm regards to yourself and officers, and wishing you all a safe and speedy return home... "[2]

The "torrid heats" of Apacheria, particularly south of the Gila river in Arizona and Northern Mexico had little effect on the Apache warrior. In the wars of the 1870s and under such conditions, it is recorded that the average American soldier "droops and dies." In contrast, it was noted the Apaches, having completely exhausted the American soldiers by ineffectual pursuit, then doubled back and were then "suddenly heard of as slaughtering and burning [the now] defenseless settlements 50 miles in rear or flank or both." (Porter, 1986:7-8)

Preparations for the raid or war
As recorded by early field workers, the Western Apache made a sharp distinction between "raiding" and "warfare."

In the case of raiding, there was an emphasis on the acquisition of material goods—mainly horses and cattle. War-parties, on the other hand, had "as their main goal to avenge the death of a kinsman who at some earlier time had lost his life in battle." (Goodwin, Basso ed., 1971:16)

Above: Return of an Apache raiding party led by the Chiricahua leader, Geronimo. Raids across into Mexico were an essential part of the Apache economy. (A drawing by Frederic Remington, Harper's Weekly, *1888)*

Below: *A rawhide container (commonly referred to as a parfleche), as used to carry "emergency rations" of dried meat or dried vegetables, on a war or hunting party. It is cut from one piece of rawhide, laced at the side, and measures approximately 12 inches x 12 inches (0.3mx0.3m). The painted designs in red, yellow and blue are on a natural white background of the rawhide itself. The curving triangular patterns and borders, together with the painted details within the main designs, suggests that this is probably Jicarilla Apache, dating from c.1870. (Taylor Collection, Hastings, U.K.)*

Unlike the Plains country to the east, the Apache terrain did not favor complete adoption of the horse for transportation.[3]

Members of war expeditions customarily traveled on foot, trusting to their well developed muscle and lung power to advance upon, or escape from, the enemy. Accoutrements and sustenance carried was minimal, to ensure rapid and unimpeded movement. Typically, a warrior packed a bow and quiver of arrows—in later years a rifle and ammunition—together with some baked mescal and small cakes of ground sunflower seeds, corn or mesquite beans. A pitched-lined wicker water canteen might also be carried. Beyond that the natural bountiful products of the desert and mountains, (and the average Apache well knew how to tap this resource) were relied upon for physical well being.

There were ample supplies of meat and vegetable produce in both the desert and mountains of Apacheria. Thus, in regions such as the Grand Canyon of the Colorado and the Rio Salado, there were Rocky Mountain sheep and down on the flatlands herds of antelope. Wild turkeys and crested mountain quail were abundant in the timbered ranges as well as in the thickets of mesquite and sage-brush. Jack rabbits were caught by encircled entrapment and even the field-rat added to the meat resource—caught by application of a knowledge of its habits and with uncanny skill using nothing more than a curved stick.[4]

In damp, elevated areas wild potatoes grew in abundance, and in addition sweet acorns, fruit of giant cactus, black walnuts and wild cherries.

Given these potential resources, an Apache warrior clothed only in loincloth, shirt and sturdy moccasins could spend days or months on raiding or war expeditions. Such were the essential physical requirements for the raid or warpath: choice of leader and spiritual support, however, were another matter.

Leaders dictated goals and tactics, but the higher powers were evoked to enhance the chances of success.

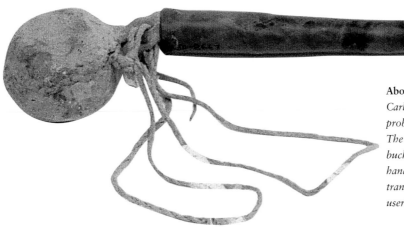

Above: *A Western Apache (San Carlos division) war club, which probably dates from at least 1880. The stone head is covered in heavy buckskin, attached to a wooden handle. The loose head reduces the transmission of shock force to the user's wrist and hand on impact.*

Below: *A San Carlos Apache twined basket water jar, which was usually pitch-lined to make it watertight. In Apacheria water was frequently in limited supply, so such items were carried by war and hunting parties.*

Training on the warpath: the Apache "novice complex"

Several students of the Southern Athapaskans have identified the existence of initiation ritual on the occasion of a youth's first war or raiding expedition. (Opler and Hoijer, 1940) Such ritual has been well documented for a number of the Apache tribes, it being reported that the novice's behavior was subjected to a definite set of prescriptions. If properly observed, it was believed that both the safety and success of the party would be assured.

This "novice complex" has been particularly well documented for the Western Apache which, as mentioned earlier, comprised the Tonto, Cibecue, San Carlos and White Mountain: a relatively large tribe of some four thousand people, who during the mid-nineteenth century occupied the region of the present-day state of Arizona.

The initiation ceremonials generally took place some four days prior to the youth—usually between the age of fifteen to seventeen—departing for his first war expedition. Instruction was carried out by a mature and experienced man. "He teaches the boy for a little while each of the four days, not all day... He just teaches him practical things that he should do on different emergencies on the raid path." (Apache informant in Goodwin, Basso ed., 1971:289-290)

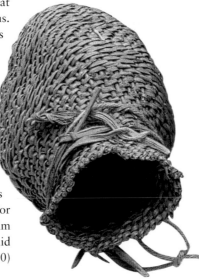

Having been instructed in practical aspects, the youth is then told of various taboos that he must observe whilst on the war or raid path. Thus, he carries a small tube made of a hollow reed and a small wooden stick. (see p.10) These are tied together with a buckskin thong and attached to the young warrior's belt. "The rule enjoined among the Apache is that for the first four times one of [the] young men goes out on the warpath he must refrain from scratching his head with his fingers or letting water touch his lips." (Bourke, 1993:40)[5] Other warpath paraphernalia was a special form of war cap. Similar in appearance to the mature warrior's war cap it differed in that emphasis was put on the use of various types of feathers. Generally four in number, they were said to impart a variety of attributes to the

novice which would be particularly useful on the war trail—hummingbird feathers for speed, quail feathers to frighten; "You know how quail jump right out from under you and scare you." (Apache informant in Goodwin, Basso ed., 1971:290) Eagle feathers were said to give protection from injury or other misfortunes whilst the small breast feathers of the oriole (generally tied at the base of the larger feathers) were described as symbolic of clear headedness—a quality "deemed essential" for success in battle. (ibid:318)

The novice was also instructed in the use of a special warpath language. This was a set of special nouns, short phrases or noun compounds which were to be employed in place of the usual, conventional forms. There were, for example, special names for mules and burros, women, Mexicans, whitemen, water, games and so on. More complex were descriptions which related to expeditions to and from Mexico. (Opler and Hoijer, 1940:620)

It was believed that violation by the novice of such taboos could cause disaster and it was recognized that no aspiring young man would want that! The obligations were all part of a very practical ethos of **rigorous vigilance** demanded of Apache individuals when they joined a war or raiding party.

Leadership in raiding and war

The most highly prized quality, for leadership in both raiding and war, was bravery and a notable record of past successes. Coupled with this, however, was the fact that such leaders were required to possess supernatural war powers, the most potent of which was described as "enemies against" power. Originally emanating from the sun, it was claimed that such powers could do miraculous things. As one Western Apache—confronted by the enemy—put it, "they shot at me [so] I said a few words to my power. 'Hold their guns up; don`t let them shoot at me. Let the bullets go over.' When I spoke these words not one of my horses got hurt, and I didn`t even hear the sounds of the bullets. In those days we used to pray in war like this." (Goodwin, Basso ed., 1971:272)

Akin to the "enemies against" power, were those derived from various animals, plants and meteorological phenomena. Thus, mountain lion powers enabled men to overcome enemies with guns

Left: A Western Apache (San Carlos division) feathered buckskin cap. There were at least five types of buckskin hats used by the Western Apache, all being related to warfare or ceremonialism. This particular hat is embellished with split owl flight feathers, and was said by one Apache informant to have been a San Carlos type. Several Apache scouts, who were employed in the U.S. Army in the wars of 1880, wore such hats. They were said to protect the wearer from harm in general and both owls and ghosts in particular—both much feared by the Apache.

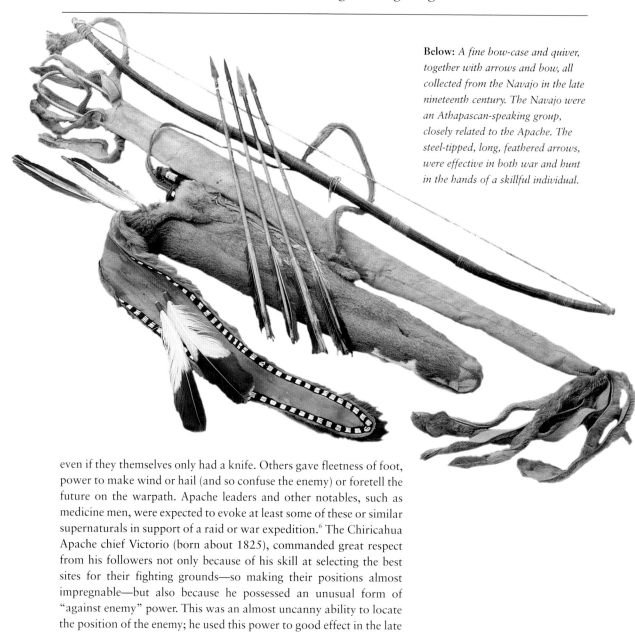

Below: *A fine bow-case and quiver, together with arrows and bow, all collected from the Navajo in the late nineteenth century. The Navajo were an Athapascan-speaking group, closely related to the Apache. The steel-tipped, long, feathered arrows, were effective in both war and hunt in the hands of a skillful individual.*

even if they themselves only had a knife. Others gave fleetness of foot, power to make wind or hail (and so confuse the enemy) or foretell the future on the warpath. Apache leaders and other notables, such as medicine men, were expected to evoke at least some of these or similar supernaturals in support of a raid or war expedition.[6] The Chiricahua Apache chief Victorio (born about 1825), commanded great respect from his followers not only because of his skill at selecting the best sites for their fighting grounds—so making their positions almost impregnable—but also because he possessed an unusual form of "against enemy" power. This was an almost uncanny ability to locate the position of the enemy; he used this power to good effect in the late

1870s when, for some fourteen months, he continually evaded, outwitted and defeated combined American and Mexican forces—even though he was encumbered with more than three hundred women and children.

As one army officer observed, Victorio provided much that all good leaders offer—psychological support for his followers. For example, during a lull in one battle "the only noise was the tom-tom beaten by Victorio, himself, all during the fight, accompanied by his high keyed, quavering voice in a song of 'good medicine'." (Smith, 1998:34)

Tactics of battle

Tactics, although ultimately determined by the leader, tended to follow several definite established patterns once the expedition was in enemy territory. Men were sent ahead to keep watch, open country was traversed at dusk, and efforts were made to reduce evidence of any tracks to a minimum. As one Apache informant commented, "Sometimes we [even] used to walk just on our toes to leave a small track. And sometimes we kept a man out behind to brush over our tracks with some bushes." (Goodwin, Basso ed., 1971:257)

Ambush was a favored method on raids, particularly near the Mexican towns. A narrow pass or gorge was selected and as the loaded wagons came through, concealed warriors would, at a signal, "start to shoot…we always had to start to fight all at the same time. Now we would kill all the Mexicans and butcher the horses or mules or oxen for meat. Then we got all the clothes and calico in the wagons to take home for our people." (ibid:258)

The distinction between revenge and raiding sometimes became blurred. Thus, on one avenge expedition into Mexico the leader of the war-party sent in four warriors to the outskirts of the garrisoned town, the rest of the war-party remaining hidden. As soon as the Mexicans saw the Apaches they retreated to the garrison to inform the officer of their presence. Chased now by the Mexican army, the four led them into ambush. The advantage of surprise enabled the Apaches to kill all the Mexicans—one warrior killed four "with just a spear." There were now few, if any constraints: "Now we all went to the town because all the soldiers were killed. When we got there we pulled the

women out of the houses by their hair and killed everyone in the town; now the chief would tell us to look for horses and cattle. We would have lots of calves, saddles, ropes, everything we wanted…we would start on our way back home, herding all our stock and packing the rest of the things we had captured." (ibid:259)

So the death of kinsmen had been avenged and, as with the raid, there was also a handsome pay off in the plunder acquired: the war-party returned doubly victorious.

Above: *Readying for ambush. From a drawing by Frederic Remington, c.1890. From a very early age, all Apache boys were taught to become skillful hunters and warriors. They were encouraged to practice with the bow, hunting birds and small game, and to participate in sham battles and foot races. This training produced individuals who, together with a keen knowledge of their environment, could survive well in harsh desert conditions. Animal-like in their stealth and patience, ambush was a favorite method of trapping the quarry, be it beast or man. In the case of the former, decoys and lures were used—here it is water, a precious water-hole in the mountains of Arizona.*

Such warfare by the Apaches made them a terror to all who came into contact with them. In the 1870s, the Mexican towns were protected by several thousand dragoons in an effort to check the depredations—but often to no avail. When pursued, the average Apache war-party seldom stood and fought but—seemingly frightened—scattered "like their own crested mountain quail." (Bourke, 1891:36)[7] Then at positions to their advantage, they surveyed the opposition, took stock and became, as a dispersed but co-ordinated efficient unit, **extremely** dangerous. As one army officer put it, "The Apache was in no sense a coward. He knew his business, and played his cards to suit himself. He never lost a shot, and never lost a warrior in a fight where a brisk run across the nearest ridge would save his life and exhaust the heavily clad soldier who endeavored to catch him." (ibid:37) This tactic was clearly the best one for an Apache warrior to adopt. Simply wearing out the enemy by frustration "the pursuit degenerat[ing] into a will-o'-th'-wisp chase." (ibid:36)

Under such circumstances Apache warriors favored higher rocky terrain. Although traveling was more difficult they had the required stamina for it, evading even the most stubborn pursuers: here too,

Left: *A Western Apache U.S. Army scout. During the Apache Wars of the 1880s, such men were recruited by the U.S. Army to track down Indian offenders. It was seen by the Apache as an exhilarating break from life on the reservation and was also a means of earning income. It was also a way in which the young, largely untried warriors could elevate their status, since the Apache war complex largely governed their behavior as scouts (see text). Army officers were much impressed with such men, admiring their sharp intelligence, keen eyesight, and great stamina in the arduous desert campaigns.*

were water holes and springs so essential for survival.

Fighting the whiteman

This guerilla-type warfare—harassing the enemy with small war-parties, ambushing and reaping havoc by rapid movement—was put to good effect in the Apache wars of the 1870s and 1880s.

Army troops generally burdened by equipment and wagons tended to follow trails on the flat lands. This type of travel made them particularly vulnerable to the Apache forces on the higher ground. Additionally, army pursuers were frequently forced to take zigzag routes so as not to lose their quarry; it was an activity which inevitably led to both exhaustion and disorientation. It was **then** that the Apache attacked.

In one such encounter "A number of simultaneous attacks were made at points widely separated, thus confusing both troops and settlers, spreading a vague sense of fear over the territory infested, and imposing on the soldiery an exceptional amount of work of the hardest conceivable sort... He is fiendishly dexterous in the skill with which he conceals his own line of march... He will dodge, twist and bend in all directions, doubling like a fox, scattering his party the moment a piece of rocky ground is reached." (Bourke in Dedera, 1971:30)

Hoddentin

Most of the Southern Athapaskans commonly used special sacred cords and headdresses to evoke the supernaturals. Less obvious, and a trait virtually unique to the Apache, was the employment of a

APACHE MEDICINE STRANDS

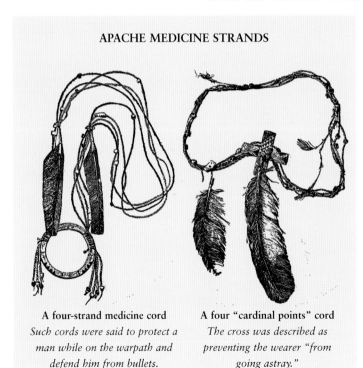

A four-strand medicine cord
Such cords were said to protect a man while on the warpath and defend him from bullets.

A four "cardinal points" cord
The cross was described as preventing the wearer "from going astray."

particular type of pollen for a variety of rituals and ceremonials — including those used for the warpath.

Generally attached to the belts of most, if not all, warriors were small buckskin bags. Some were ornamented, others were plain. They were handled with great care, containing a yellow powder to which the Apache gave the name *hadntin* or *hoddentin*. This powder has subsequently been identified as the pollen of the tule , a cat-tail rush found near water holes in Apacheria.

Hoddentin was considered an important component in ceremonials, to cure the sick. At intervals between chants, it was applied by the medicine man to the forehead of the patient, then on the chest and finally it was sprinkled to entirely encircle the patient. Attention was now turned to those who, by chanting or otherwise, were supporting the medicine man in his endeavor to cure. These too were similarly 'blessed' by the powder. *Hoddentin*—rather like the blessed water of Christians—had wide applications. It was used in the Puberty ceremonial of Apache girls, sprinkled on a corpse and used as a restorative on exhaustive marches. In some way it was considered to evoke the higher powers to good effect, it being reported that "the very first thing an Apache does in the morning is to blow a little pinch of *hoddentin* to the dawn." (Bourke, 1993:51)[8]

So important was *hoddentin* in ceremonies of a religious nature amongst the Apache, that an expression *hoddentin schlawn* came to mean "that a particular performance or place is sacred." (ibid:57)

Little wonder then that the Apache warrior seldom set out without a bag of the precious powder attached somewhere on his person — generally on his ammunition belt. On starting out, a pinch of *hoddentin* was offered to the sun, a pinch was also put on the tongue and the crown of the head and "When they return, they hold a dance, and on the morning of that day throw pinches of *hoddentin* to the rising sun, and then to the east, south, west, and north, to the four winds." (ibid:51) To the *hoddentin* was added the feathered and beaded medicine strands, the warcap and the "enemies against" power. All this combined to ensure success in raiding and war.

Clearly, the renowned war prowess of the Apache warrior depended not only on personal resilience and skill, but also on the psychological support that was gained by these appeals made to

Above: *A small beaded pouch of buckskin, decorated with seed beads, probably Jicarilla Apache. These were carried on the belt or at the throat. Small bags of this type could be used to carry hoddentin or hadntin. This has been identified as the pollen of the tule, which grows in the ponds and cienegas of the southwest. Army officer Captain John Bourke—who had an unusual interest in Apache culture—reported in 1887–88 that, "No Apache would... go on the warpath without a bag of this precious powder somewhere upon his person." (Bourke, 1892:51) (Taylor Collection, Hastings, U.K.)*

CHAPTER IV

Wakan`yan

("By my supernatural power" - Lakota)

The Way to Status:
Early Plains Indian Warfare

"Without war an Indian is no longer an Indian. War is his
means of educating himself. Success in war is his supreme aim
in life. By nature imperious and full of energy, he finds in
martial exploits his only chance to win distinction. In
renouncing war he gives up his chief life purpose; he is forced to
rearrange the plan of his whole existence."
(Kurz, Hewitt, ed., 1937:295)

Below: *A view of the Great Plains in
northern Montana—home of the
buffalo and the Plains Indians. Vast
areas were largely devoid of trees or
significant natural barriers. However,
there were beautiful river valleys,
wooded regions and outcrops where
the Plains Indians lived well.*

COVERING A LAND AREA of almost one million square miles, the
Great Plains are the very heartland of North America. Its
approximate boundaries are defined by the Mississippi—Missouri
valleys to the east and the Rocky Mountains to the west. In the south
it ends at the Rio Grande in New Mexico and Texas. At the north
edge, the boundary is the Saskatchewan river of Alberta and
Saskatchewan. As one scholar has put it, this is a "land of sun and
wind and grass." (Wedel, 1961:20)

This vast region is largely devoid of significant natural barriers which gives free play to air currents. Some areas experience ocean-like winds, icy from the northwest in winter and hot from the south in summer. Locally—summer or winter—conditions can suddenly change, a "norther" can plummet the temperature by 50°C and the sky blackens with a frightening intensity. Winds can be a gentle breeze, then, within minutes, change to a ferocious gale with chaos in its path.

Man and animals have to rapidly adapt to such conditions—or perish. As one scholar has observed of Plains animals, many exhibit several characteristics which strongly reflect the "nature of the country" and serve "as an index to the problems of [living on] the Plains." (Webb, 1931:33) Thus all, with exception of the wolf and coyote, are grass-eaters and all can survive for an extended time without water. Most are extremely difficult to approach and kill, whilst some, such as the jack-rabbit and antelope, are amongst the swiftest four legged animals on earth.[1]

Such characteristics—resilience, strength, speed of movement and marked ability to survive—were also the attributes and skills of those Indian groups who from prehistoric to historic times peopled the Great Plains. During the latter period in particular, these people were known for their great vitality and lived with a vibrant intensity. They had an acute awareness of all around them, a great wonder of the power of the sky, land and animals and virtually all were believed to have a spiritual existence. As has been previously observed, "There was an awareness of a great force—the Sioux called it *wakan*—distinct from physical power which could act in different ways for good or evil and there were few Plains warriors who did not endeavor—often by great personal sacrifice—to possess and control at least part of it." (Taylor, 1975:10)[2] Such power was earnestly sought to enable success on the warpath.

Below: *The pronghorned antelope, considered amongst the purest type of Plains animal, roamed the Great Plains in vast numbers. Their keen sense of sight enabled them to detect danger over immense distances and they are amongst the swiftest four-legged animals in the world. The Cheyenne, and other historic Plains tribes, hunted the antelope by use of specially constructed pits or ditches, which were similar to the buffalo pound.*

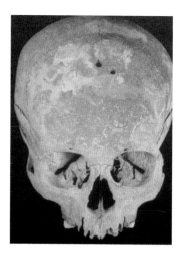

Above: *A skull from Iowa, perhaps one thousand years old, and below, illustration after Owsley and Jantz eds., 1994. They all show evidence of scalping and the use of a skull as a trophy.*

Changing military skills and tactics

As has already been mentioned, a study of both the archeological and historic record has led to an identification of four major phases of Plains Indian warfare tactics, each emphasizing a variety of skills. (Smith, 1938; Lewes, 1942; Secoy, 1966; Ewers, 1975) Prehistoric and then (approximately in the period 1650–1750) post-horse pre-gun on the Southern Plains, paralleled by post-gun pre-horse on the Northern Plains. The third phase—undoubtedly the most dramatic and intense period of intertribal warfare—was when both the horse and gun frontier met: this combination created a formidable equestrian gun-armed foe. The fourth phase—which is considered in the final chapter of this book—is the approximate period 1850–1890. This was a time of increasing conflict between the Plains tribes and Euro-Americans, as the latter moved inexorably west—the Plains Indian-White confrontation period. (See Chapter VI)

In all four phases the reasons for going to war and the tactics employed were generally markedly different. Thus, in the case of motivation for conflict, a major emphasis in prehistoric times was undoubtedly an increasing demand for access to the bountiful resources of the Great Plains as well as more desirable territory.[3] This motivation was, it appears, not infrequently driven by changing climatic conditions; it led to some particularly brutal encounters,[4] such as at Crow Creek in present-day South Dakota where some five hundred men, women and children were annihilated. This, and other sites which have been excavated in recent years by archeologists, indicates that not only were individuals extensively mutilated—cranial fractures, decapitation and the removal of various body parts—but some were also scalped.[5] (Robarchek in Owsley and Jantz, eds. 1994:335). Women too were carried off by the victorious war-

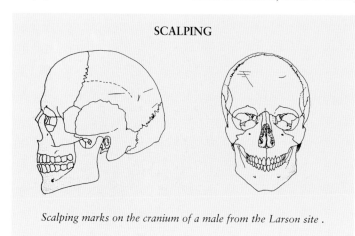

SCALPING

Scalping marks on the cranium of a male from the Larson site .

riors. They were prized not only for their child-bearing capacity but, in this pre-horse period, as vital burden-bearers, particularly when the camp was on the move.[6]

Shield-bearing warriors

The tactics employed and the accoutrements carried and worn in this prehistoric phase of Plains warfare can be reconstructed not only by the pictorial evidence offered by petroglyphs and pictographs but also by the observations recorded by early explorers such as David Thompson (c. 1780) and Lewis and Clark (c. 1804). Most dominant in the early petroglyphs and pictographs are depictions of large shields being carried by pedestrian warriors. Additionally, they are shown wearing elaborate headgear, the most noticeable feature of which is the use of buffalo horns. Heavy clubs, spears, lances and long bows are in evidence as well as the use of coup sticks. The shields are often shown embellished with elaborate geometric as well as realistic designs. Clear evidence that, even at this early period, there was emphasis on evoking of the spirits to protect the shield-bearing warrior. The very real mechanical protection afforded by the heavy rawhide from which the shield was fabricated was thus reinforced by an appeal to higher powers.[7]

At this period too, as with tribes to the east, such as the Iroquois and Huron, body armor was also worn. The pictographic record is unfortunately lacking as regards a definite image of such human body armor. However, there is one particularly good description from the explorers, Lewis and Clark, who in the summer of 1805 met up with a band of Shoshone near the Missouri river in present-day western Montana. They noted that the warriors wore a "kind of armor, something like a coat of mail, which is formed by a great many folds of dressed antelope skins, united by means of a mixture of glue and sand. With this they cover their own bodies and those of their horses, and find it impervious to the arrow" (Hough, 1893:646). Such tribes as the Shoshone and Kutenai had dominated the Northern Plains for aeons prior to the western movement of the Blackfeet. Lewis and

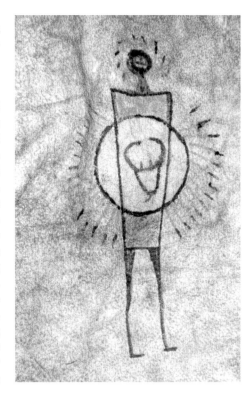

Above: *Pictograph of a pedestrian shield-bearing warrior, Northern Plains, c.1800. Heavy rawhide gave protection from arrows or spears but not the gun! Additional protection was sought by symbols drawn on the face of the shield. This one shows a buffalo head—buffalo power—and a fringing of feathers, probably eagle, around the edge. (From a robe in the National Museum of Ireland, Dublin, Specimen No. 1882, 3881. Photograph by author.)*

Clark`s description is clearly of skilfully fabricated protective garments which had been used for centuries in Plains warfare—well before the introduction of the horse and gun.[8]

Infantry tactics and skills

A graphic description of one style of pedestrian warfare was recounted in 1797 by an aged Piegan chief, *Saukamappee*, "The Boy." He told the explorer David Thompson of a battle between some three hundred and fifty Piegan warriors and a somewhat larger force of Shoshone. This took place about 1725 near the Eagle Hills just west of present-day Saskatoon in Saskatchewan: *Saukamappee* was then 16 years old. He described in some detail not only infantry-style tactics employed by both sides but also the nature and effectiveness of the weapons used and he refers to pre-battle ritual.

Although it is clear that the opposing forces were intent on counting coup and taking scalps, they initially took up a stance of lines facing one another and were barely within arrow range. Protection was by means of large shields about 3 feet (1m) in diameter. Much show had been made prior to this encounter—"singing and dancing"—and arrangements were made for some shields to "shelter two men." There was a great deal of consideration of the fire power on both sides; the Shoshone had short sinew-backed bows and flint-tipped arrowheads. The sinews, *Saukamappee* reported, made the bows "very elastic and the arrows whizzed about them as balls do from a gun."

Although the Blackfeet bows were longer, their range was apparently limited. However, their arrows were tipped with iron points which stuck into the rawhide shields of the Shoshone whilst their flint tipped arrows shattered on impact. Clearly, there were advantages and disadvantages on both sides and a closer encounter was avoided. Although several were wounded, none were actually killed, *Saukamappee* wryly reporting that the "night put an end to the battle, without a scalp being taken on either side, and in those days such was the result, unless one party was more numerous than the other." (Thompson, Tyrrell, ed. 1916:328–329)

Below: *"Spearing the enemy" pictograph on a Lakota (?) buffalo robe, c.1830. This is one of eight war episodes depicted on this particular robe. The leader wears an eagle feather headdress, the feathers erect—a common style of head regalia for this period. He carries a war-pipe and large scalp in his left hand. Both war and hunting scenes were depicted in pictographs by many North American Indian tribes, although the Plains tribes excelled in this art form. (Museum of Mankind, British Museum, London, Specimen No. 917. Photograph by author.)*

Left: Wahktägeli, or *"Gallant Warrior,"* a Yankton Sioux chief. *Referred to as "Big Soldier" by the American traders, he was painted in his full regalia by the Swiss artist, Karl Bodmer, in May 1833. His costume is embellished with porcupine quills and beads, the hair fringe on his shirt reportedly having been made from the heads of Mandan enemies. His elaborate hair ornament, of feathers (some painted) and red cloth, makes reference to enemies slain in battle.* Wahktägeli *was an impressive man and nearly 6 feet 6 inches tall (1.9m). He was about sixty years old when this portrait was painted.*

Saukamappee hints at the possibility of a more bloody outcome if one side had superior numbers. Such an encounter was observed by members of the Spanish Onate expedition to the Southern Plains in the early 1600s. Here some fifteen hundred Plains Apache confronted a much smaller enemy group (probably Wichita). The pedestrian warriors now used a technique of extending their infantry line as long as possible, moving forward towards the enemy. As they did so, the line became gradually concave, the outer warriors moving ahead thus encompassing and virtually surrounding the opposing force. Massive showers of arrows rained down on the enemy and the Wichita were slaughtered to a man.[9]

Above: *Scalp decorated with beads and porcupine quills c.1830—one similar was carried by the Mandan chief, Four Bears. (Blackmore Collection, Hastings Museum, U.K. Photograph by author.)*

Below: *"Scalp Dance" celebrating the return of a Cree war-party. (Peter Rindisbacher, c.1820.)*

Changing warfare patterns: the impact of the gun

By about 1740 a limited number of guns were becoming available by trade to the Blackfeet, via the Cree and Assiniboin, who had in turn acquired them from the Hudson Bay posts to the east.[10] This weapon significantly changed the balance of power on the Northern Plains. Again, the aged Piegan chief *Saukamappee* relates an unsurpassed eighteenth century description of the Blackfeet-Shoshone struggle in their attempt to dominate the vast regions encompassed by present-day Saskatchewan, Alberta and northern Montana.[11] He relates the usual pre-battle display

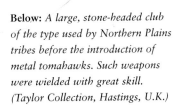

of numbers, weapons, and shields. In particular, he describes the Shoshone as carrying stone-headed clubs wielded with great dexterity. "It was," he said, "a dangerous weapon" in close combat. A note of foreboding creeps in. The Shoshone were being directed by a tall chief "and had they [then] made a bold attack on us, we must have been defeated as they were more numerous and better armed than we were." The Piegan war chief, however, adroitly directed that the guns were to remain hidden. Until the time was ready, they were thus kept in "their leathern (buckskin) cases."[12]

Now the Shoshone formed the "long usual line," placing their shields on the ground and each war chief encouraged his men to stand firm. The young *Saukamappee* commented with a hint of dry humor, "and most of us waited for the night to make a hasty retreat!" But now the Piegan chief—anxious to see the effect of the new weapon—directed those with guns to stand in the front line. Each carried two spare balls in their mouth and a quantity of powder in the left hand for reloading. The line moved forward to within 60 yards (approx. 60m) of the Shoshone who, with their powerful sinew-backed bows and superior numbers, clearly felt the advantage. Raising now from behind their rawhide shields, they drew their bows. So exposed the Piegan "fired with deadly aim" and either killed or severely wounded "every one we aimed at."[13] Appalled at finding so many of their numbers now disabled or dead by the devastating fire, the Shoshone stayed hidden behind their shields. The lull gave the Piegan a chance to reorganize the infantry formation, spreading two gun carriers at intervals along the front line. Clearly as one fired, the other was reloading. This newly acquired skill with firepower "caused consternation and dismay" amongst the Shoshone warriors and several started to take flight. Seizing the advantage, the Piegan war chief urged his men forward, leading the charge with spear in hand. Whilst most of the Shoshone ran for their lives, a number stood their ground, they "fought bravely and we lost more than ten killed and many wounded." (ibid:330–332)

Such were the tactics and skills in pedestrian Plains Indian warfare but it would never be quite the same again. Although the Shoshone and their allies had actually acquired the horse before the Blackfeet, they failed to develop any efficient cavalry skills to counter the

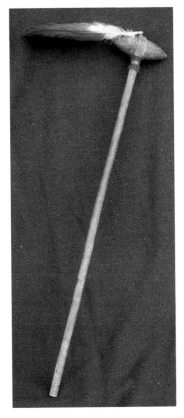

Below: *A large, stone-headed club of the type used by Northern Plains tribes before the introduction of metal tomahawks. Such weapons were wielded with great skill. (Taylor Collection, Hastings, U.K.)*

advantage of their gun-armed opponents. Thus, the former dominant military alliance on the Northern Plains—Shoshone, Kutenai and Flathead—gradually retreated west, settling on the Plateau. However, they continued for a generation or so to make surprise raids (now on horseback) to capture Blackfeet and Cree women. These they traded to the Comanche and others for European goods.[14]

Guerrilla warfare

The disastrous battles experienced by the Shoshone and their allies against the gun-armed Blackfeet and Cree radically changed the nature of intertribal warfare. The Shoshone avoided pitched battles and the infantry-style formations—as described earlier—and now they put emphasis on surprise attacks, large war-parties attempting to destroy small encampments completely. It required skill of stealth, as well as patience and endurance, to get within striking distance of such villages (many of which were guarded by dogs) but the vengeful Shoshone honed their guerrilla warfare techniques very efficiently. As *Saukamappee* commented:

"They have the power to vex us and make us afraid for the small hunting parties that hunt the small deer for dresses and the Big Horn for the same and for Bowls. They keep us always on our guard." (ibid:340) Recognizing the dangers, the Blackfeet now began to gather in larger camps. Although this was undesirable for any length of time (since it rapidly depleted local resources), such a concentration of population ensured that the guerrilla tactics were less successful. As the explorer Alexander Henry observed in the early 1800s, "In summer [the Blackfeet] were obliged to assemble in large camps of from one hundred to two hundred tents, the better to defend themselves from enemies." (Henry and Thompson, Coues, ed., 1897:723)

Thus, the gun not only changed military techniques but it required reorganization of living styles in order to ensure efficient and effective use of the new and bountiful resources that the Great

Below: A Blackfeet horse raiding party in warm weather dress. Such raiding parties generally set out on foot. A little dried meat was carried, but usually food was procured on the way. A pack carried spare moccasins, a sewing kit and possibly a small robe for bedding. These parties consisted of the war leader and warriors, together with a "kettle bearer" and scout. (Sketch by Calvin Boy. From Ewers, 1955.)

Above: *Blackfeet encampment, Brulé Flats near Fort McKenzie, Upper Missouri. This scene was painted by the Swiss artist Karl Bodmer, in the summer of 1833. It shows the circular formation of tipis used by the equestrian tribes, for protection from enemy attack. At the left foreground is a warrior wearing a painted robe, showing his exploits in war and the hunt. Wolflike dogs abound—these were important guards against the stealthy enemy.*

Plains offered. More so when the horse impacted on the region. Similar adaptability occurred on the Eastern Plains. Tribes such as the Cheyenne and Teton Sioux (who prior to the 1650s lived beyond the Mississippi and were largely a horticultural people) were progressively driven west by the gun-armed Chippewa. The warfare styles employed by such tribes at this time were Woodland in character (see Chapter II). Thus, on meeting the enemy, forces tended to be immediately scattered, individual warriors taking advantage of "the best nearby cover and still effectively support each other by fire." (Secoy, 1953:68)

When the Teton Sioux moved west they were confronted by vast expanses of treeless terrain of which *Saukamappee* had commented, "we were at a loss what to do on the wide plain ...our chief encouraged his men to stand firm." But this was a tactic alien to Woodland warfare. Thus, when a Sioux war-party attacked the rear guard of a war-party of Cree, to the former's dismay they were now suddenly

Left: Quaneh *Parker, one of the last great war-chiefs of the Comanche. Chief of the Antelope band of the Staked Plains region, he was one of the last to surrender to the United States authorities. It was a surrender, in June 1875, which ended war on the Southern Plains and opened up their traditional homelands to the advancing frontier. Quaneh Parker was born about 1847—his mother was a white captive, Cynthia Ann Parker. Of strong character and sharp intelligence, he has been described as the greatest Comanche chief of all time. Kwahnah (Quaneh) is Comanche for "Sweet Odor." (Painting by Frank Humphris. Taylor Collection, Hastings, U.K.)*

confronted by some five hundred warriors from the main body. Alarmed and surprised they now scattered and took flight, abandoning a portion of their arms so as to reach the shelter of an isolated wood. Now, more confident in familiar surroundings, they held off the Cree until nightfall "the Cree in the open like brave men, the Sioux hiding behind trees." (Burpee, ed., 1927:136) All that changed, as gun-armed Siouan and Algonquian tribes filtered into the Northern and Central Plains and even more so when the gun frontier finally met the horse frontier in the mid-eighteenth century.

Comancheria warfare tactics on the Southern Plains
From about 1300 to 1700 it was the Athapaskan speaking Apaches—known in the historic period up to 1800 as "Padoucas"—who held sway on the Southern Plains. This tribe, together with their Navajo cousins, had migrated from the far north about 1200. Aggressive warriors and hunters, they ransacked the villages of the relatively peaceful and ancient inhabitants of the region. By circa 1660 these people had both horses and metal weapons: the new resources and skills led to an expansion of intertribal warfare which ranged far and wide. (Hyde, 1959)

A generation or so later, however, the equestrian Comanche, a sub-tribe of the *Gen du Serpent* or Snakes (Shoshone), began to move south from the Plateau region. Rapidly adopting Spanish-style cavalry equipment, modifying their warfare techniques, and always on the move they systematically ransacked and destroyed—mainly by utilizing the element of surprise—the Apache horticultural rancherias.

Later to be termed "Lords of the Southern Plains" it was the Comanche, together with the Kiowa who, with little opposition, now dominated the region. One much-impressed traveler to Comancheria was a certain Joseph Farnham who, in the early 1800s, described the Comanche as the "Spartans of the Prairies" noting that "their incomparable horsemanship, their terrible charge, the unequaled rapidity with which they load and discharge their fire-arms, and their insatiable hatred make the enmity of these Indians more dreadful than that of any other tribe of aborigines." (Farnham, In Wallace and Hoebel, 1952:34)

73

Below: Wild horses on the Southern Plains, from a sketch by the artist and traveler, George Catlin, in 1834. Generally referred to as mustangs, they roamed the region in large herds. The capturing of such animals was considered a mark of great skill by the Southern Plains tribes—particularly the Comanche, who were considered amongst the best horsemen on the Plains. This tribe became exceptionally skilled in both hunting and warfare tactics, which were almost exclusively carried out on horseback. (After an engraving by George Catlin. Taylor Collection, Hastings, U.K.)

The mustang

A major source of horses on the Southern Plains, either by trading or raiding, were the Spanish settlements in New Mexico. Another source, however, were those which were captured from the wild herds which roamed the region.

Generally referred to as "mustangs" (derived from the Spanish for stray or feral) they were common on the Southern Plains. Thus the traveler, George Catlin, commented in 1834 that the "whole country" (in the vicinity of present-day Oklahoma and Texas) "seemed at times to be alive with ...bands of wild horses." (Catlin, 1926, Vol.II:63) The Southern Plains tribes in particular viewed the capture of wild horses as an important measure of skill. In the case of the Comanche, lassoing "gave young men a real chance to show off and gain prestige while enjoying an exciting sport." (Wallace and Hoebel, 1952:42) Other methods used to capture the mustang were by using corrals, ambushing at a water hole, or "creasing."[15]

A major advantage of the mustang was their great endurance, speed and marked ability to survive. Mustangs were efficient foragers, subsisting in winter on little but bark and twigs. Such attributes were greatly admired by the Plains Indian.

Stealthy warriors: stealing the best horse

Although the capture of wild horses was considered a measure of skill, actually stealing horses from the enemy was even better. As one authority on the Comanche observed, they were "the top horse thie[ves] of them all." (ibid, 1952:44)

Taking horses under difficult circumstances provided the opportunity to display cleverness and unsurpassed valor. A distinguished mark of honor amongst the Comanche—a type of coup—was the stealing of horses and those "most successful in this enterprise were highly respected" (ibid.:44). The lengths to which a Comanche horse thief went to were a source of astonishment to army officers. Thus, Colonel R. Dodge recorded that the Comanche could crawl into a "bivouac where a dozen men were sleeping, each with a horse tied to his wrist by the lariat, cut a rope within six feet of the sleeper, and get away with the horse without waking a soul." (Dodge, 1877:401)

Comanche horsemen

George Catlin was obviously greatly impressed with Comanche horsemanship. He recorded on his visit to a large village of that tribe (in 1834) that they were "the most extraordinary horsemen that I have seen yet in all my travels, and I doubt very much whether any people in the world can surpass them." (Catlin, 1926, Vol.II:74) Hence, the development of skilled pre-gun-post-horse warfare techniques on the Southern Plains: as has been described earlier, it created—particularly in the case of the dominant Comanche—masterly warriors.

On horseback, and with adept use of just bow, lance and shield they could, in their quest for war bounty, outwit and, if necessary, destroy the most formidable of foe.[16]

There was, however, a limitation to their effectiveness due to the paucity of guns and a regular supply of ammunition. It was not until the late eighteenth century that the Comanche had access to a dependable supply of fire power: fully two generations after they acquired the horse.[17]

Above: *Capturing horses from the Crow Indians, a sketch drawn by the Hunkpapa/Sans Arcs (Lakota) warrior and medicine man, known to the whites as "His Fight" (although Oki'cize-eta'wa translates better to "His Battle" or "The Battle's Own.") In his early days, His Fight was known for his success in capturing horses and he was something of an authority in war customs. He was particularly adept at illustrating war and hunting exploits in pictographic form. In the upper sketch a single horse is captured in a Crow encampment. It is clearly the owner's favorite, as it is picketed next to his tipi. The lower sketch shows a herd being run off; the warrior is dressed in a wolf- or fox-skin headdress—a popular guise for scouts.*

CHAPTER V

Hokahey!
("Lets go" - Lakota)

Impact of the Horse and Gun on the Plains Indians

"A powerful and warlike people, haughty and defiant—well over six feet in height, strong muscular frames and very good horsemen, well dressed, principally in skins and robes; rich in horses and lodges; have a great abundance of meat since buffalo, elk, antelope and deer abound in their country. They say they are Indians and do not wish to change their way of living" (S. Latta, Indian Agent Upper Missouri. c. 1860)

WHILST THE FRONTIER of the horse progressively extended from the Southern Plains, that of the gun moved west and south from the Woodland region. The introduction was slow; the more western tribes greatly depending on middlemen as a source of supply.

Right: A detail from an early robe, collected c.1840. The robe was identified as belonging to a "Sioux chief" and it depicts some of the various important episodes in the owner's life. These included activities both in the hunt and war. In this particular scene, the chief is shown wearing a red military coat, carrying a lance and shield and beating a gun-carrying warrior. (Friedrich Kohler Collection, Museum für Völkerkunde, Berlin.)

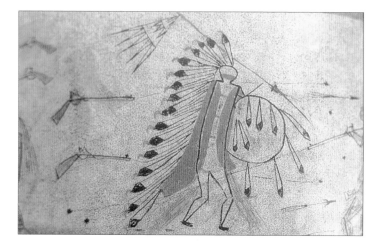

The Sioux attained their first guns from the Huron and Ottawa. These tribes, as with the Iroquois further east, had long been active in the fur trade. By the 1650s they were trading a few guns and metal goods—knives, axes, tomahawks—to the Sioux. The supply, however, was limited since there was an underlying hostility between the Sioux and the eastern tribes, the latter having no inclination to arming potential foe as they sought to dominate the fur trade in the region. Within a generation or so, however, (by the 1680s) French traders redressed the balance enabling the Sioux to attain a steady supply of guns from the east.[1] Now as gun-armed—but pedestrian— warriors and hunters they pursued aggressive expansionist activities both in war and trade. Sioux groups such as the Teton (Lakota) moved westward exploiting a virgin terrain which was rich in animal life—not least beaver. Beaver pelts were now directly traded to the French in return for guns and ammunition. By the last quarter of the seventeenth century the Teton Sioux had largely abandoned a horticultural lifestyle for pedestrian nomadism.

Hunting for horses

The movement of other tribes, who were later to become the equestrian nomads—the Plains Indians known to history—was similar. Thus, such tribes as the Arapaho, Cheyenne and Crow all migrated to the Plains region from the northeast under the relentless pressure of gun-armed Woodland Indians. In 1680, for example, the Cheyenne occupied the region of present-day Illinois, but by 1700 they were on the Cheyenne River in present-day southeastern North Dakota—more than five hundred miles north-west of their original homelands. Here, they were living in permanent earth lodge villages leading a dual life of nomadic hunting in summer and residency in the earth lodges during the winter. This lifestyle persisted for at least two generations but then, about 1770, they were attacked by a force of some one hundred and fifty gun-armed Chippewa. The village was

Below: The Cheyenne warrior, Wolf Robe—the very epitome of a Plains warrior. The Cheyenne were unsurpassed as both hunters and warriors and bitterly opposed white subjugation which, they knew, would change their lives for ever. Finally, they capitulated subdued by gun-armed opponents and their massive resources.

Above: *A gun-armed Chippewa (Northern Ojibwa), c.1820. Identified as Chief Peguis, this portrait is by the Swiss artist, Peter Rindisbacher. Such superior-armed warriors confronted the various Sioux tribes in the late eighteenth century, pushing them westwards onto the Plains. Chief Peguis carries, in addition to the "thunder-stick," traditional weaponry such as bow, club and knife.*

destroyed mainly because many of the occupants "had just gone out hunting on horses" (Jablow, 1950:8)—the horse had arrived on the Central Plains!

"They die under the burden"

In pre-horse days women, as already mentioned, were amongst the major spoils of war being considered highly valuable not only for their child-bearing potential, but also for their burden-bearing abilities. One observer who visited a Kansa village in the early 1700s made reference to the fact that both dogs and women were capable of transporting loads of up to 300 lbs. (approx. 140 kg.). This staggering weight, he observed, caused "difficulty [in] marching" (Ewers, 1955:142). As tribes became increasingly richer in trade goods, acquisition of the horse clearly became a major necessity. As one Pawnee chief said, "[We want to] obtain horses which will help us to carry our belongings when we move to our winter grounds, because our wives and children die under the burden when we return" (ibid:142-143).

The raid for horses

Unlike dogs, which were owned by the women, the majority of the horses were generally owned by the men; there was, however, a considerable imbalance in horse wealth amongst the Plains and Plateau tribes. Figures varied considerably in the nineteenth century but in the 1870s, tribes such as the Nez Perce and Cayuse on the Plateau, had a horse-person ratio of more than seven whilst the ratio was just under three for the Kiowa, Comanche and Blackfeet. For many others it was 1:1 or less and some tribes, such as the Cree and Assiniboin, were still very dependent on the dog.[2]

Old tribal alliances—Blackfeet, Assiniboin, Cree who formerly united against the Shoshone in pre-horse days—changed with the Assiniboin and Cree now raiding the Blackfeet for horses. Well armed with guns obtained from white traders but poor in horses, they coveted those of the Blackfeet. The reverse was not true: tribes knew who had good and plenty of horses and they were selective against whom they carried out horse raids. Blackfeet attacks on the Cree and Assiniboin were more for revenge than for fine horses.[3]

Below: *An exploit of White Grass, a Piegan chief (c.1870). Here he is entering a Flathead encampment, to cut free two picketed horses. He also captured the enemy chief's bow, arrows and quiver.*

Similar patterns emerged on the Central and Southern Plains. No conflicts between Crow and Blackfeet prior to 1810 changed with the mobility of the horse and Sioux-Crow warfare after 1855 or so, centred primarily around the raid for horses although if the opportunity for scalp-taking occurred, it was not passed over. Scalps now generally became tokens of success, the scalp-lock only being removed and used to embellish costume and horses. Scalping did not necessarily

Above: *A whistle made of the wing bone of an eagle and embellished with ribbons and feathers. These instruments were used in the Sun Dance and on the battlefield. They were said to imitate the cry of an eagle, imparting courage to the warriors. It is recorded as early as 1807 that war leaders hung these around their necks when they rode into battle. (Taylor Collection, Hastings, U.K.)*

kill, but there are well recorded taboos relating to the status of a scalped person even apparently at this time.

Organization of a raid for horses was a complicated affair not only involving war ceremonial, war songs and war-pipes but also the nature of winter and summer kits, the wolf headdresses for the scouts and the food which could be carried. Then there were the complexities of the homeward journey which, as recorded for the Comanche, could be with several hundred captured horses—although it was recognized that it was dangerous to be too greedy. Afterwards there were the post-raid ceremonials, the distribution of the captured animals and booty, a consideration of the status accrued and obligations defined—all a pathway to successful leadership.

There were some definite similarities between the early slave raids and later horse raids. In both cases travel was on foot. Because only limited equipment could be carried, knowledge of where the war lodges were located was essential. It was from here that the leader directed operations—clearly the war lodge was important for shelter, as a base for scouting, supplies, and information (Ewers, 1968:128)

Leadership in the quest for horses was without question a big responsibility and even some of the best men cracked under the pressure. Thus, it is related that one Kiowa leader lapsed into "some type of schizophrenic condition, obsessed with the delusion that all of his men were horses" (Mishkin, 1966:33). One day he stopped the party, lined up the warriors and examined the teeth of each man. Another day he forced all of them to bray in chorus, threatening to shoot any of them if they did not comply. This, on the face of it an amusing incident, led to disaster. The party was ambushed and all but completely annihilated. The raid for horses was a dangerous venture and war-party members had to keep their wits about them to survive!

Organization of a war-party
Such intertribal warfare, particularly the raid for horses, allowed Plains warriors to expend their emotions to the full. Their "Dionysian" personalities—tense, creative and with positive, strong attitudes—found, without question, free play in the horse raid.

An efficient leader generally selected his war-party carefully and the role of supporting personnel was not overlooked. Thus, a well organized group of perhaps between ten to fifty often included youngsters who were not yet of warrior age and possessed no 'medicine'. They joined the expedition as apprentices, their work mainly concerned with preparing the food, looking after captured horses and generally making themselves useful. Occasionally, women would also go along, especially those who had no children. They rendered valuable service in mending worn clothing, particularly moccasins. Except for a little dried meat, no food was taken as this could be procured on the way; each man carried his own wooden bowl or large horn spoon from which he could eat or drink. The war leader, as he was called if he personally possessed the necessary supernatural power to give some guarantee of success, and had not sought the help of another, appointed assistants who acted on his behalf.

The two most important posts were those of "kettle-bearer" and scout. The "kettle-bearer" not only organized the cooking arrangements but also took care of "certain eating and drinking customs which were common features of war party practice" (Smith, 1938:440). For example, the great Cheyenne war leader, Roman Nose, possessed medicine power which forbade the eating of food which had been cooked in an iron vessel, and only after elaborate purification ceremonials could a violation of that rule be rectified.[4] The "kettle-bearer" might also be entrusted with the care of the War Medicine Bundle. The scout took on the practical role of locating the enemy and protecting the war party from surprise attack.

Tracking the enemy—skills on the warpath
Mapping
Early observers of the Plains tribes reported on the geographical expertise that many of them possessed. The fur trader, Edwin Denig, for example,

Below: *A small container made of rawhide, commonly referred to as a parfleche. Such containers were used to hold dried meat and berries, as required for use on the warpath or on hunting expeditions. They were tough, light-weight and waterproof. Many were highly decorative, with distinctive geometric designs. Probably Crow, dating from c.1870. (Taylor Collection, Hastings, U.K.)*

Below: *The war chief* Mato-tope, or *"Four Bears," a portrait by Karl Bodmer, 1834. Four Bears' outstanding exploits are illustrated by his elaborate hair ornaments of feathers and carved sticks.

reported that the Assiniboin—a tribe he knew well—were both capable and accurate in rendering the topography of their country.

In December 1853 he obtained from an Assiniboin warrior a detailed and well scaled map of the area, north and west of Fort Union as far as Fort Benton and was further moved to write, "In conversation with most elderly Indians regarding locations, travels, or to explain battles and other events, resort is had by them to drawing maps on the ground, on bark with charcoal, or on paper if they can get it, to illustrate more clearly the affair in question. In this way the chief of the Crow Nation three years since made and left with us a map of his intended travels during the entire fall and winter succeeding, embracing a circumference of 1,500 miles, with the different encampments to be made by that nation in that time, and so correct was the drawing that we had no difficulty in finding their camp the following winter in deep snow, one month's travel from this place" (Denig, 1930:605).[5]

Travel at night was helped by observation of the stars, the North Star in particular was familiar to most Plains tribes and in times of heavy cloud the direction of the wind helped in indicating the correct course towards the enemy. Rivers were crossed by use of bull-boats, if time permitted, otherwise a small

makeshift coracle of hide and sticks to carry clothing and powder only was employed by the swimming warriors.

Acute perception: reading the signs

Enemy signs could tell much. Thus, camp fires would tell the number of persons; the condition of the ashes and horse droppings, remains of meals, the terrain—broken or bent grass—and tracks by water's edge would indicate how recently occupied. Tribal identity might be confirmed by observation of discarded and worn out moccasins, arrowheads, even a bead or two. A skilled Indian scout could, by consideration of all these factors, assess with remarkable accuracy most of what he wished to know.

Old time Plains Indians had acute sight. "At a distance of 12 or 15 miles they will distinguish animals from timber, even supposing they are not in motion. If moving they will discern between horses and buffalo, elk and horses, antelope and men, a bear and a bull, or a wolf and a deer, etc. But the greatest mystery is how they make out anything living to be there at such a distance, on the instant, when they themselves are in motion and the animal at rest. This they do when it is surrounded by a hundred other objects as like to living creatures as it is. Once pointed out, the movements are watched and its character thus determined. Their powers in this respect are truly astonishing and must be acquired. They also judge very correctly of the relative distances of objects, either by the eye or to each other. Smoke can be seen rising on the plains at a distance of 60 miles, and they will tell from that or any lesser distance within a few miles of the place where it rises" (ibid:528).

A well developed system of signalling was employed both to convey information to distant members of the war-party and on return to those in camp. A forward scouting party, on sighting the enemy,

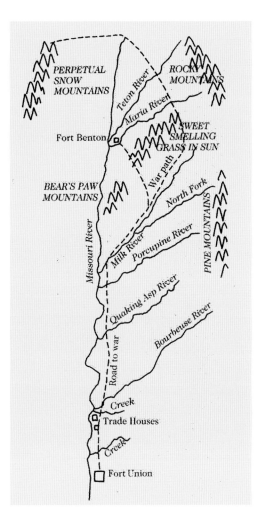

Above: *Map drawn c. 1850 by an Assiniboin, showing the route of a hunting/trading trip on the Upper Missouri. American Indians often drew maps for use in war and hunt.*

Left: *Typical geometric designs for a Lakota pipe-bag, c.1880. The designs are skillfully worked in trade seed beads and sewn in place on sinew threads. The lower part, just visible, shows slats of rawhide bound with red, white and mauve porcupine quills. The **meaning** of such designs could only be obtained by reference to the maker. When the anthropologist, Clark Wissler, interviewed Lakota craftswomen in the early 1900s, he found that they frequently referred to geometric designs of this sort in terms of hunting and warfare episodes. Lines indicated the flight of arrows; projecting points, arrow wounds. The beaded red spots, hits or wounds. Rescue episodes and dead enemies were also documented. The red rawhide strips made reference to blood. (Taylor Collection, Hastings, U.K.)*

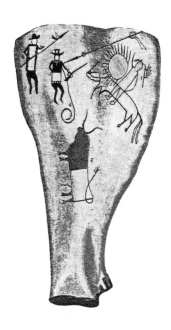

Above: *A painting on a buffalo scapula, found in Comanche country, c.1850. Messages were left by war and hunting parties; they were rendered pictographically on birch-bark, rawhide and also, as shown here, on bone. An advantage of the latter would be that the scapula could be pushed into the soil. The message seems to make reference to a conflict between an Indian and two Mexicans (or Spanish) over a domesticated bull (note the lyre-shaped horns).*

commonly conveyed this intelligence to the main group by rapidly riding backwards or forwards or in a circle; blanket signals were also commonly employed and mirror signals were particularly popular. Often the system to be used was first discussed and agreed; thus there was no universal code although the discovery of a large band of enemy was commonly conveyed by vibrating the mirror, giving a continuously moving beam. Smoke signals were employed in a similar way but according to one reliable authority they were used in a very limited manner by Plains Indians (Clark, 1885:415).

Messages

It was not unusual for war-parties to leave messages for their members who scouted ahead or were following. Many comments of early observers of Plains Indians indicate that picture writing and a system of signs was well developed and understood. On leaving camp, Blackfeet war-parties frequently left a willow stick bent V-like and stuck in the ground, the apex pointing in the direction taken. Stragglers or other parties would know that if the angle was acute, the distance to the next camp was small. More precise instructions were frequently left by a kind of map marked on the ground. The V symbol was again employed to indicate direction, rivers and streams were mapped out, whilst pebbles coloured black or pieces of charcoal marked the proposed camping places, the number in each case was to indicate the resting time. "In cases where the stops were by day and travel by night, yellow pebbles were used instead of black," and the fact that two parties had joined was indicated by V-shaped symbols converging (Wissler, 1911: 43).

The messages were, of course, doubly useful; not only did they convey information to warriors actively engaged in the same war expedition, but if the war-party was overdue it would be possible for searchers to follow the sequence of events.[6]

The war lodge

The first camp made after leaving the confines of the village was considered particularly important for it "reflected the substitution of the road of war for that of peace" (Smith, 1938:442). Such a camp might be quite close to the village; as well as having religious significance it also served as a base for both pre-battle and post-battle ceremonials; here the outward party performed some of the necessary medicine power obligations to ensure success, and on return prepared for a ceremonial victory entrance to the village.

Nearer to enemy territory, war lodges were commonly used by war-parties. These were permanent structures of wooden poles set somewhat like those of a tipi but closer together. On average the poles were some 12 feet (3.6m.) long and tied at the top. Lighter poles were leaned against the foundation poles and the whole framework was usually covered with slabs of cottonwood bark. The lodge was entered through a passage-way barely 4 feet (1.2m.) high and 10 feet (3.2m.) or more long. "Informants said that in the time of their youth there were a great many war lodges in the country of the Blackfeet and their enemies. The lodges were located in heavily timbered areas near rivers or streams, or on thickly wooded heights, conveniently near well-known war trails. There were many along the Missouri River, and it was the business of leaders of Blackfoot war parties to know where they were located" (Ewers, 1968:118).

Not only did the war lodge provide both protection from enemy attack and unpredictable weather, it also served important functions as a supply and information base and was an important part of the Plains Indian war complex.[7]

Vows for success

As they neared the enemy, and anxiety and tension increased, Sioux warriors commonly pledged the Sun Dance vow. Such times would surely be a moving experience to any observer for these hardy warriors of the Plains were also sensitive, family loving people. Many had children, relatives and friends who they dearly wished to see again. "They felt that no extreme of heroic endurance would be too great an expression of thankfulness if they were reunited with their friends"

Below: *A small paint pouch, c.1880, probably Blackfeet or Assiniboin. The bag is buckskin, and the beadwork sewn with fine sinew thread. The red motifs probably represent horse tracks. There is personal war or hunting symbolism here, but it has gone unrecorded. (Taylor Collection, Hastings, U.K.)*

(Densmore, 1918:101). *Mato'kuwa'pi*, "Chased by Bears" spoke such a vow for his party: "Just before sunrise I told the warriors to stand side by side facing the East. I stood behind them and told them to raise their right hands. I raised my right hand with them and said: '*Wakan'tanka*, these men have requested me to make this vow for them. I pray you take pity on us and on our families at home. We are now between life and death. For the sake of our families and relatives we desire that you will help us conquer the enemy and capture his horses to take home with us. Because they are thankful for your goodness and will be thankful if you grant this request these men promise that they will take part in the next Sun Dance. Each man has some offering to give at the proper time'" (ibid:97).

Some warriors performed personal ceremonies before a battle, such as the famous Crow chief, Rotten Belly, with his shield which was said to have powers of prophecy. The Crow warrior, Blows Down, was the owner of a sacred hoop which was also believed to possess prophesying powers. He describes holding the hoop in the rising smoke of sweet grass—upon looking into the hoop, he and his companions saw a vision of many horses (Wildschut, Ewers ed.,1960:46).

Power of the war paint

Ideally, before going into battle, warriors painted their bodies and faces and at times their horses as well, the designs being in accordance with dreams or bestowed by some successful warrior. The painted design on the body was generally considered a form of protective power—painting was seldom done purely for ornament. The Omaha, for example, "When going to battle, on the surround at the tribal buffalo hunt, when taking part in the Hedewachi ceremony, at the races, at the Hethushka society, and the Pebble society, the

Above: Nowayke-Sugga, *an Otto Indian, c.1830. The headdress of dyed deer hair and woven headband of wool and beads, is typical of this tribe, and the Iowa and Winnebago. The bear claw necklace is indicative of prowess. (McKenney and Hall print. Taylor Collection, Hastings, U.K.)*

Below: *Horses painted for battle and parade.*

Right: *Appaloosa, dressed for parade celebrating war or hunting exploits.*

1. Cheyenne/ Lakota. Horns of prong horned antelope refer to swiftness and survival powers of one of the purest Plains animals
2. Cheyenne. Dragonfly symbolic of whirlwind and associated with the thunder and rain spirit. Protective.
3. Cheyenne. Pony painted with motifs symbolic of wounds received, point of impact and bleeding emphasized.
4. Blackfeet. Pony with figure of man on chest, symbolising that a man was ridden down in battle by the owner of the horse.
5. Blackfeet. Painted with symbols of former battles to arouse courage and enthusiasm for war.

painting on their faces and bodies had a serious significance, partaking of the nature of an appeal or prayer" (Fletcher and La Flesche, 1911:350).

If time permitted, warriors might seek the services of a man who specialized in making war medicine. Thus, *Tasun-ka-wakan*, "Holy Horse," painted four warriors' faces brown with a white line across the forehead which extended down the cheek and forked at the end. He also painted their horses with white clay "drawing zigzag lines from the mouth down the front legs, branching at the hoofs, and the same on the hind legs; there was also a band across the forehead and spots on the chest" (Densmore, 1918:353). As he painted the men and their horses, Holy Horse sung the following song concerning the paint:

le	this
maka	earth
wecicon kin	I had used as paint
on	causes
oya te	the tribe (of the enemy)
ini han waye lo	much excitement

(Song Concerning War Paint, sung by *Siyaka*, ibid:353-354)

1   2   3   4

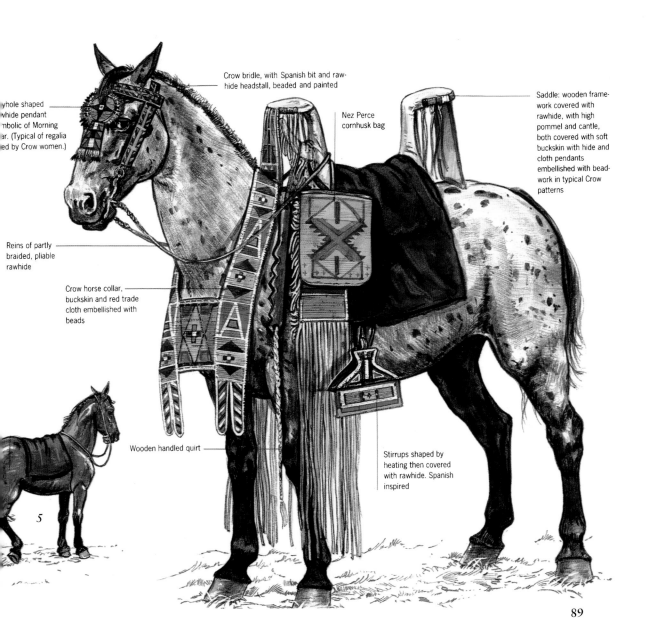

yhole shaped
whide pendant
mbolic of Morning
ar. (Typical of regalia
ed by Crow women.)

Crow bridle, with Spanish bit and rawhide headstall, beaded and painted

Nez Perce
cornhusk bag

Saddle: wooden frame-
work covered with
rawhide, with high
pommel and cantle,
both covered with soft
buckskin with hide and
cloth pendants
embellished with bead-
work in typical Crow
patterns

Reins of partly
braided, pliable
rawhide

Crow horse collar,
buckskin and red trade
cloth embellished with
beads

Wooden handled quirt

Stirrups shaped by
heating then covered
with rawhide. Spanish
inspired

5

89

The painting on both horse and man was representative of *Wakinyan*, the lightning or thunder spirit so respected and feared by the Plains tribes. On the treeless plains the death-dealing qualities of lightning were terrifyingly apparent—animals and men were often struck. Thunder Power and the horse were commented on by the anthropologist, Clark Wissler: "The horse always appealed to them as a creature of mysterious origin , and in many cases was assumed to have been given by the thunder. In any event there is an association in their minds between the power of a war-horse and the thunder" (Wissler, 1907:46).

War paint sometimes led to interesting episodes in the life of a warrior, such as in the case of the Hunkpapa, Rain-in-the-Face. When a young man, he joined a war-party which successfully captured horses from the Gros Ventre; the party found themselves pursued and it was necessary to make a stand. Rain-in-the-Face painted his face to represent the sun "when halfcovered with darkness – half black and half red." Fighting for a whole day in the rain his face became streaked with the red and black war paint which confirmed his boyhood name of Rain-in-the-Face (Hodge, ed., Vol.II 1910:353).

Capturing the favourite horse

The Plains tribes seldom guarded or corralled their horses unless there was evidence that the enemy were in the vicinity. By hobbling the lead mare and selecting good pasture it was generally possible to contain the herds overnight within a comparatively small area. Youths were often given the task of daily caring for horses and it was they – at the instructions of the owner – who drove them to pasture at night and retrieved and watered them the next day. There was no central responsibility from the band leaders or council, it generally being recognized that each family was responsible for his own herd.

Although the majority of horses were largely unguarded at night, a significant exception was that the favourite and best horse was commonly picketed outside the owner's tipi. The capture of such a horse in the very heart of the enemy's camp required both skill and courage. It was an objective which most ambitious warriors sought for; not only did it guarantee a quality animal but such a deed ranked highly in the scale of recognized war honours. Further, it sustained a

Above: *The noted Hunkpapa (Lakota), Rain-in-the-Face, from a portrait by the artist DeCost Smith, August 1890. Rain-in-the-Face was a leading participant in the Little Bighorn Battle of June 25, 1876. A man of considerable warrior distinction, he received his name due to streaked war-paint on his face.*

Right: *The Wet, a Crow chief, from a painting by DeCost Smith on the Little Bighorn, in 1890. This distinguished man was associated with a dramatically described episode when a Lakota warrior tried to capture his horse, which was picketed adjacent to his tipi (see text). He wears an ermine-fringed shirt, which is now in the collections of the Field Museum of Natural History, Chicago.*

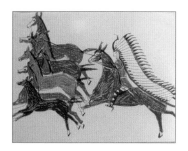

Above: *Capturing Crow horses, as depicted by the Lakota warrior, Wanblí waha cunka, "Eagle Shield," who also rescued his injured leader.*

"game" element which so characteristically threaded its way through Plains Indian intertribal warfare. But it was a dangerous game. The artist, DeCost Smith, has left us a vivid description of an abortive attempt by a young Sioux warrior to capture the favourite horse of a prominent Crow warrior known as "The Wet."

"Fully awake now, fully alive to the situation, with his eye at the peephole, he felt for his rifle and raised it noiselessly to be ready. Outside a tall form had just cut the lariat, made a half hitch around the horse's jaw, and was starting to lead it away. Quickly, with soft, swift tread The Wet stepped over the threshold, and with the muzzle of his gun almost touching his enemy's back, fired. The horse started at the flash; the man fell. Instantly The Wet shouted his coup cry 'I, The Wet, have just killed an enemy. I am first to strike.' Bird Head then struck the dead man, and, finding his gun at the same time, announced in a loud voice his claim of second to strike an enemy, and first to capture an enemy's gun" (Smith, 1943:145-146).[8]

Post mid-nineteenth century, intertribal warfare became largely synonymous with the horse raid. Close contact with the enemy was generally avoided, although – as has just been related in the case of the unfortunate young Sioux warrior – face to face encounters inevitably occurred. A widespread attitude throughout the Plains at this time was summarized by a noted scholar of the Plains Indians, George Bird Grinnell when he wrote: "there were many brave and successful warriors of the Cheyennes... who on their war journeys tried to avoid coming in close contact with enemies, and had no wish to kill enemies. Such men went to war for the sole purpose of increasing their possessions by capturing horses; that is, they carried on war as a business – for profit" (Grinnell, 1923, Vol. II:2).

The victory dance
With the possible exception of the Arikara,

(Smith, 1938:443), all successful war-parties made camp before entering their home village. Here they prepared for a grand entrance and the subsequent rejoicings in the form of victory and perhaps scalp dances. Here, warriors could go carefully over their war exploits, rehearse their victory songs and dances, don their war dress – all for the maximum dramatic effect. Then, approaching the village they rode in singing their war songs.

The return of a successful war-party was an occasion for rejoicing and celebration, the victory dances and recounting of war honours which were acted out in a dramatic and realistic fashion, putting emphasis on the superiority of the group over the enemy. Generous warriors gave away captured horses, thereby elevating their prestige further. Such actions "served as a stepping-stone to leadership" (Ewers, 1955:189).

If scalps had been taken then, and this was undoubtedly embedded in the early lore of the tribes, returning warriors rode into camp with faces painted black, shooting their guns into the air and carrying the scalps on long poles. "The people were excited, and welcomed them with shouts and yells. All was joy. The women sang songs of victory...In the front rank were those who had...counted coups...Some threw their arms about the successful warriors. Old men and old women sang songs in which

Above: *Return of a successful Cheyenne war-party, as in c.1870. The shield is embellished with typical Cheyenne symbolic motifs. (Watercolor by Tom Lindsey, Taylor Collection, Hastings, U.K.)*

their names were mentioned. The relatives of those who rode in the front rank...testified to their joy by making gifts to friends or to poor people. The whole crowd might go to where some brave man lived, or to where his father lived, and there dance in his honor... They were likely to prepare to dance all night, and perhaps to keep up this dancing for two days and two nights" (Grinnell, 1923, Vol.II:6&21-22).

Such a returning Assiniboin war-party was observed and sketched by the Swiss artist, Rudolph Kurtz, in 1851 and even after the time that the scalp raid took on a minor role, Sioux warriors still continued to sing war songs containing the phrase "the black face paint I seek" (Densmore, 1918:359), and definite rituals were observed in its use. Thus, Sioux war-parties which had defeated the enemy without loss to themselves allowed not only the first four who had killed enemies to use the black face paint but it could also be used by their women relatives who participated in the scalp dance.

The changing role of women in Plains warfare

The greatly reduced demands for women as burden-carriers due to the availability of the horse, led to a marked shift away from the practice of slavery. This also extended to the symbolic concepts associated with scalp-taking; the changes occurred rapidly – in less than a generation.

Women as warriors

Women themselves might now actively engage in warfare. As the Sioux anthropologist, Beatrice Medicine remarked, with the coming of the horse a warrior role was not then considered an unwomanly one but simply an alternative which she "might accept if she so chose" (Albers and Medicine, 1983:274-275).

Amos Bad Heart Bull records an outward bound Oglala Sioux war-party consisting of six men and two women who carried packs on their backs as did the men (Blish, 1967:172). It is highly probable that they were wives of the men

Below: A drawing showing an outward bound Oglala (?) (Lakota) war-party of six men and two women, pictured by the young Lakota historian, Amos Bad Heart Bull, c.1890. As the late, distinguished ethnologist, John C. Ewers observed, there is ample evidence that a number of women, of many tribes, joined raiding parties and took active parts in them. (Ewers in Owsley and Jantz, eds., 1994:328) Here, the war-party is leaving the home camp on foot. The partisan (leader) carries the consecrated pipe and the two women at the rear carry packs on their backs, as do the men. A note, in Lakota on this drawing translates as "women also go along." (From Blish, 1967:Fig. 88)

on the expedition and were in the capacity of helpers. Many women now became expert on horseback and there are several accounts of successful female leaders of war-parties. Good examples of such female leaders were Woman Chief, of the Crow, who was reported on in considerable detail by the trader, Edwin Denig, in the 1850s, and the Piegan woman, Running Eagle, who became the heroine of one of James Willard Schultz's novels.[9] The Blood Indian, Weasel Tail, said that the men who followed her on the warpath respected her highly and she was particularly successful in raiding for horses of the tribes west of the Rockies. Weasel Tail also said, however, that she always insisted on cooking for her war-parties and indeed mending their moccasins. When the men protested she replied, "I am a woman. Men don't know how to sew" (Ewers, Owsley and Jantz, eds., 1994:329).

The late John Ewers told me of a Piegan woman whom he had

Below left: *Minnie Hollow Wood, a Sioux lady, photographed c.1890, one of the few women in her tribe who had the right to wear a war bonnet—a distinction attained after combat against the U.S. cavalry.*

Below: *Winyan Hanska, or "Big Woman" (Oglala). Her red wool dress commemorates her brother capturing horses and the two hands refer to the battle where he was killed. (Painting by Paul Ritner, after a photograph by Weygold, 1909. (Taylor Collection, Hastings, U.K.)*

known in the 1940s. She accompanied her husband on several war-parties, capturing trophies from the enemy. We speculated that Annie Bear Chief must have been amongst the last of the nineteenth century Blackfeet women to have been involved in such war activities.

Women on the battlefield

Portrayals of women in action against their enemies are fairly rare. However, Father Nicolas Point makes reference to, and illustrated, a young Pend Oreille woman who led a party of men of her tribe in the destruction of a Blackfeet war-party (Peterson and Peers, 1993:73). Bad Heart Bull also documents the case of a Cheyenne girl who, on a spirited horse,

Above: *Cheyenne girl at the Battle of the Rosebud, June 17, 1876. She accompanied her brother into battle and the encounter was subsequently known among the Sioux as the "Fight Where the Cheyenne Girl Showed Great Courage." Portrayal of women in action against their enemies is quite rare. This episode so impressed the Lakota historian, Amos Bad Heart Bull (who made this sketch, c.1900), that the red crosses which he marked on the battlefield map are said to show the places where she performed particularly well. (From Blish, 1967:Fig. 104)*

entered the strife at the Battle of the Rosebud in June 1876. She did so in company with her brother, her courage apparently arousing the admiration of all who saw her. Red crosses on a map drawn of the battlefield by Bad Heart Bull are thought to mark the places where the girl performed particularly well (Blish, 1967:188). Apparently the Rosebud Battle was quite commonly known among the Sioux as the "Fight Where the Cheyenne Girl Showed Great Courage" (ibid:189).

Clearly then, the woman warrior role was a far cry from the pre-horse days of women as burden-carriers and trophies, the woman`s place in this respect being firmly replaced by the horse. Little wonder that capturing horses became a major war activity of the Plains Indian and much encouraged by women! The recognition that some women could take on the role of warriors, however, was something of a double-edged sword. Now women, sometimes even children, might be killed rather than captured during intertribal warfare. As Denig observed in the mid-nineteenth century, "the Assiniboin, Blackfeet, Sioux, Cree, and Arikara also kill women and children and sing and dance as much for their scalps as for those of men" (Denig, 1930:552).

There were some notable exceptions to this custom, such as with the Crow who, small in number, captured women and children to strengthen the tribe. Other exceptions were on a more personal basis such as the case of Joseph White Bull (nephew and later adopted son of Sitting Bull) who spared the life of an Assiniboin woman because she reminded him of his mother. Her "take pity plea" resulted in the woman, her husband, and White Bull's war-party picnicking together with a firm warning not to wander on Sioux territory again! (Howard, ed., 1996:47).

Changing accoutrements, changing skills
Horse equipment

With increasing wealth in horses, new indigenous technologies were developed amongst Plains Indians who became expert in fabricating their own equipment leading to greater proficiency in both the hunt and war. There was a lively trade in those parts made of metal, particularly bridle bits which in early days mainly came from the Southwest hence having an obvious Spanish influence. However, as pointed out by Wissler, much was distinctly Plains Indian.[10] For example, there was extensive use of rawhide and expert techniques in its application. In the 1830s, Catlin illustrated one of several methods employed by the Plains tribes in the fabrication of horse equipment, when he visited a Comanche village (probably Kwahadi) west of the Washita River. He shows a saddle frame covered with wet rawhide and pegged to the ground to dry (Wissler, 1915). Later, sinew, threads and cords would subsequently be used to skillfully secure the rawhide permanently in place. Bone, buffalo hair, rawhide, sinew and porcupine quills have been used to produce a magnificent saddle, which is now in the Liverpool Museum, England.[11]

Indigenous artwork was adapted in decorating ceremonial parade equipment, such as pad saddles and high pommel and cantle women's saddles. For more than a century and a half, great emphasis has been given to an elaborate display of horse equipment and accoutrements – particularly by the Blackfeet and Crow – a custom still admired and appreciated.

Body armour

As mentioned earlier, defensive weapons – armour and shield – were often massive in pre-horse days. On horseback, however, there was a demand for greater mobility and by the late eighteenth century (1790

Below: Cree crupper, c.1840. As the equestrian culture developed on the plains, horse equipment became increasingly elaborate. This crupper, made of buckskin backed with trade cloth, is embellished with porcupine quillwork. At least five different quill techniques have been used on this piece. (Taylor Collection, Hastings, U.K.)

Left: *Crow Indian horse equipment, c.1880. The metal bit, with the heavy copper chain fringe at its lower end, is a trade item much coveted by the Crow. It was generally referred to as a "Spanish cheleno." The attached bridle is made from a recycled parfleche, and is heavily beaded. The whole is typical of Crow work for this period, as is the keyhole-shaped head ornament, displaying a Morning Star motif. An old label states that this was formerly the property of Sitting Bull—quite believable, since at this period, Sioux and Crow were trading extensively. (Taylor Collection, Hastings, U.K.)*

or so) the equestrian tribes were wearing an attenuated multilayered style of body armour, some with sleeves down to the elbow, as reported for the Yankton Sioux by Peter Pond (Innis, 1930:58). Others, such as those described for the Shoshone, Blackfeet and Plains Apache, were sleeveless, some painted red, green or blue. Such garments probably looked something like that worn by a Tonkawa warrior sketched by Lino Tapia in 1829 (Berlandier, Ewers ed., 1969:Plate 5). Hide armour was also used on horses as well as men; it was effective against arrows, far less so against the gun. When the Sioux abandoned armour because it no longer gave mechanical protection it persisted in a single-layered decorated form and symbolic of high-ranking office – that of a shirt-wearer. Similar changes occurred in the case of horse armour, a highly decorated caparison taking its place.

The shield

On the Northern and Central Plains, shields were progressively reduced in size for use on horseback, now being about 18-20 inches (45-50 cm) in diameter rather than 30 inches+ (75 cm+) as was the custom with seventeenth century pedestrian warriors. On horseback the attenuated shield was generally carried on the left arm to cover the vital parts, at the same time leaving the hands free to handle offensive weapons. The heavy rawhide could stop an arrow and deflect or deaden the ball from a muzzle-loading flintlock. However, with the introduction of high-powered guns and an emphasis given to the horse raid rather than scalp raid they were seldom carried on the warpath. Token protective emblems remained – such as carrying the shield cover or models of the full sized shield often painted with designs which were believed to give protection to the owner. The use of the large shield appears to have persisted longer on the Southern Plains and pictorial evidence from George Catlin and others indicates that such shields were in vogue and carried by both pedestrian and equestrian warriors. As with the lance, the retention

Above: *Pictograph, c.1830, by the Mandan chief, Four Bears. A distinguished second-chief of the Nuptadi Mandan, he was credited with great mastery of Mandan religion and ceremonial, and as a skilled hunter and resourceful warrior. The pictograph techniques he developed are distinctive for their realism and detail. This figure shows one of some twelve battles documented on a large painted buffalo robe, which is also decorated with porcupine quilled bands and disc. (Courtesy, Linden Museum, Stuttgart, Specimen No. 36125a)*

of such defensive weaponry may have been due to Spanish influence in this region.

The spear and lance

As *Saukamappee* reported for the Shoshone-Blackfeet battle in the 1720s, the lance was commonly carried by foot warriors. With the acquisition of the horse it fell into disfavour on both the Northern and Central Plains – although there were several notable exceptions. Sitting Bull`s favourite weapon, for example, was a lance given to him by his father and the Blackfeet were known to have used them on occasions even as late as the 1860s.[12] Long lances and long bows, so popular in pre-horse days, were now replaced with the bow-lance and generally now considered more as a society emblem than a weapon.

This was not, however, the case on the Southern Plains where the lance continued to be a favourite weapon long after the acquisition of the horse. It is probable that direct contacts with Spanish-Mexican soldiers, who were trained and skilled lancers, may well have encouraged greater use of the weapon by the Southern Plains. Berlandier describes the use of the lance for both the Plains Apache and Comanche; they could be up to 12 feet (3.6m.) long and frequently

Left: *Equestrian warrior, in combat with a pedestrian opponent, drawn on a small deerskin in brown paint. This may be an episode in the life of* Thatha´ka Iyótake, *"Supreme Bull," known to the world as Sitting Bull. The hair-style and moccasins of the pedestrian warrior suggest he is a Pawnee. Although expert with bow, knife, war club and tomahawk, it is recorded that Sitting Bull favored the lance. The description of his lance matches the one shown here. (Museum of Mankind, British Museum, London, Specimen No. 1954 967 W.AM.5. Photo by author.)*

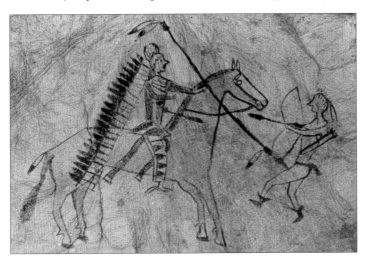

had a blade some 30 inches (75 cm) long which was fabricated from a Spanish sabre (Berlandier, Ewers ed. 1969:130). Unlike the Spanish lancers, however, the Southern Plains tribes when using the lance never adopted the Spanish one-handed method: instead the two-handed overhead thrust was generally employed which was undoubtedly a survival from pre-horse days.[13]

The tomahawk

The pipe tomahawk was early used in the east – illustrations of "smoak tomahawks" (as the English called them) going back to at least 1796 (Taylor, 1997:27). The ease with which such a combined weapon and pipe could be carried on horseback led to a very considerable demand for such weapons by equestrian warriors. Now, the heavy catlinite pipes and stone-headed war clubs were largely replaced by a relatively light-weight and double use instrument. Ingenious styles were developed in the main, it seems, by local blacksmiths who could respond quickly and readily to changing tastes.[14] These metal tomahawks were employed somewhat differently and wounded differently to the widely used stone-headed war club which had been in use for hundreds of years by pedestrian nomads. As *Saukamappee* related, this latter weapon was devastating in the hands of a resolute warrior. With a head having a mass up to 6.5 lbs. (3 kgs.), the momentum acquired during rotation crushed skull and bone on impact. When used on horseback, the additional

Above: *An Osage war axe, c.1850(?), which belonged to the distinguished chief* Washin-ha. *The handle is covered with a red cloth with a trade wool selvedge edge pendant (typical for this region), with eagle feathers and bells. Early accounts record that, like the ball-headed club, tomahawks were thrown with "utmost dexterity" and "unerring and deadly aim." (Catlin, 1926, Vol. 1:266)*

Above: *Sioux warrior, c.1860, wearing a turban-like headdress with eagle feathers. His metal tomahawk has a smoking bowl. (Copy of early photograph collected by William Blackmore, c.1870. (Taylor Collection, Hastings, U.K.)*

Below: *Typical Plains Indian bow and arrow. Skillfully used, such weapons could bring down a 2,000 lb. (900kg.) buffalo more efficiently than a gun. (Courtesy Neil Gilbert Collection, Suffolk)*

forward velocity would increase the momentum still more, causing greater devastation – although the weapon must have been difficult to handle under these conditions.[15] Easier was the lighter weight metal tomahawk which cut rather than crushed, being deftly wielded in an axe-like fashion.[16] It was a weapon much favoured by equestrian warriors whilst the stone-headed club now became a popular ceremonial item often much reduced in size and weight and elaborately decorated.

The bow

Long bows – so popular in eastern North America – were also used by early Plains tribes. Such bows were certainly a feature of pedestrian warfare; later they were then markedly reduced in size, it has been contended, for easier use on horseback. Such a step, however, is not crucial to efficient use by equestrian warriors, historians documenting that medieval English-style long bows were used very effectively on horseback.[17] Likewise, the Comanche, "cousins" of the Shoshone (who used short bows), actually used relatively long bows made from Osage orange which was available to them from the eastern Prairie region. Perhaps it was a combination of factors which led to reduced sized bows, not least availability of suitable woods. As Roland Bohr noted, "Only rarely were the inherent qualities and capacities of certain materials for bowmaking and their availability taken into consideration. Trees growing on the Great Plains clearly show the influence climactic extremes, [characteristic of the region], had on their growth. Knot-free wood of sufficient length and straightness for making longbows was and is hard to come by on the Great Plains." Thus, Northern and Central Plains tribes in particular would be "forced to abandon their longer

bowdesigns in favor of shorter bows while they moved farther West as long bow wood became increasingly scarce." Sinew backing, as Bohr observed, enabled serviceable bows to be made from short pieces of wood and they were very effective against long bow users who initially relied on local woods as they pushed into the Plains region (R.B. Personal Correspondence. July 1999).

Saukamappee illustrates this point in his descriptions of early battles between Blackfeet and Shoshone. The pedestrian Blackfeet employed bows some 5 feet (1.6 m.) in length which were made of larch wood. When confronted by the Shoshone who had short sinew-backed bows, the arrows were described as being cast with a greater force than those of the Blackfeet. Both Shoshone and Blackfeet were on foot. The implication is that short bows were adopted because they were superior to the long bows made of larch, the only wood

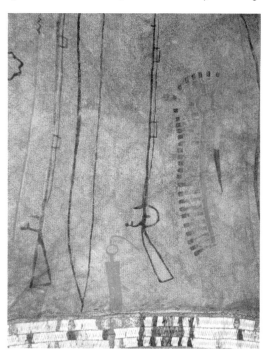

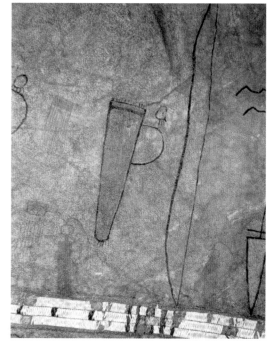

which grew on the Plains and which was knot free and straight – but it was an inferior material.[18] Thus, the adoption of the horse did influence the change from long to short bows. However, it was probably not because short bows were easier to use on horseback but because the equestrian tribes now found themselves in a terrain which no longer yielded the necessary materials for the traditional long bow.

Swords and sabres
Unlike the Southern Plains tribes who favoured the sabre blade as a head for their lances, the Central Plains tribes not infrequently used the sabre or sword itself either as a weapon or as a status symbol. Thus, early pictographic robes collected from such tribes as the Sioux, Cheyenne, and Mandan depict warriors carrying swords or sabres on horseback and employing them in battle to good effect.[19] These scenes are relatively early (before c. 1840), but it is clear that the sabre was still a popular weapon a generation or so later.

Recently, attention has been drawn to the sabre-wielding Cheyenne warriors in a series of pictographs (Afton, Halaas and Masich, 1997). These sabres/ swords were obviously used with great skill both as weapons and to count coup. Some modifications took place; the manufactured knot, for example, was generally replaced with long strips of otter fur tastefully shaped and generally painted on the flesh side. Swords and sabres were apparently important trade items as James Hanson of the Museum of the Fur Trade, Chadron, Nebraska, has observed: "I've seen lots of illustrations, both drawings and photos, of Indians with swords. Most of them appear to be English Model 1796 light cavalry swords, surplussed after the

Above: *A series of arrowpoints of a type used on the Northern and Central Plains, from the prehistoric to the late historic period. Arrowheads were carefully crafted to match the quarry. That at the left, with the long point, was for large game such as buffalo and wapiti; the other two metal points are also designed for hunting, the tangs are serrated to ensure that the head remains on the shaft during extraction. A war point generally had a smooth tang so that it slid off the shaft when attempts were made to extract it. The three stone arrowheads are of the type used prior to the introduction of metal. (Taylor Collection, Hastings, U.K.)*

103

Napoleonic wars. They sold them all over the west, including at the Bordeaux Post in the late 1830s and 1840s. However, I have not seen anything on their actual use in battle, except in pictographs, and cannot recall a written reference to their use. Perhaps they were more like society regalia, or for show like knife clubs. Maybe it was to imitate soldiers, the Long Knives" (J.H. Personal Correspondence. August, 1999).[20]

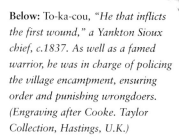

Additionally, many swords and sabres were ordered directly from London and elsewhere, becoming something of a status symbol. In the case of the Sioux, strangers taken under the protection of high-ranking warriors, were symbolically guarded by a sword or club placed by the entrance of the lodge. It has been reported that such signs were "well understood, and no Indian ventures to intrude" (McKenny and Hall, 1933, Vol.1:416). Likewise with the Crow, where the sword and lance progressively became a symbol of a high-ranking equestrian warrior. In parades, the weapon was now carried in an elaborately decorated rawhide case, often by the wife or close female warrior – a tribally recognized statement of success and valour.

Below: To-ka-cou, "He that inflicts the first wound," a Yankton Sioux chief, c.1837. As well as a famed warrior, he was in charge of policing the village encampment, ensuring order and punishing wrongdoers. (Engraving after Cooke. Taylor Collection, Hastings, U.K.)

Protective and other amulets associated with the horse

Riding with heavy rawhide shields was not very practical. The Crow warrior, Two Leggings, for example, reported that the persistent rubbing of the carrying strap caused considerable discomfort (Wildschut, Ewers, ed., 1960:65). Further, as mentioned earlier, the shield gave little mechanical protection from high-powered rifles.

Various styles of light-weight amulets were now much favoured by the Central and Northern tribes – such as a 5 inches (13 cm) model Crow shield and a hair-lock which belonged to the Blood Chief, Red Crow. This latter is possibly part of the Blackfeet Catchers` Society Bundle, it being the only part of

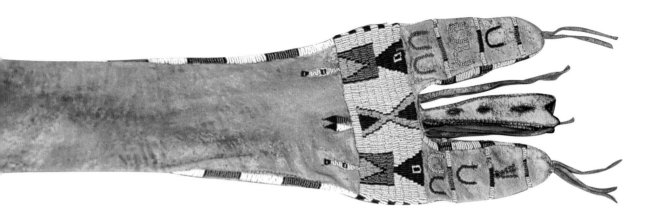

the Bundle worn on the warpath representing the potency of the Bundle to ensure success. Other war medicines were more personal, such as the beaded horse effigy which has been identified as a Crow Horse Capturer's charm.

Successful horse raids were documented in a variety of ways, such as the moccasins which belonged to Many Roads, a Hunkpapa Sioux who lived at Standing Rock. They are replete in symbolism referring to horses captured as well as the terrain and weather travelled through. Likewise, a pipe-bag embellished with numerous horse tracks has been associated with a successful horse raid leader.

Of particular interest in this category is a neck ornament which formerly belonged to the Blood Indian, Good Striker. It is decorated with an array of horse teeth and diamond-shaped pieces of mica attached to beaver or otter fur. The teeth are smeared with red paint – always indicative for the Blackfeet of a sacred object. Good Striker's war exploits have been well documented and one particularly successful war-party which he led, raided a Crow camp on the Yellowstone River where many horses and guns were captured. As yet it has not been possible to relate this unusual ornament to any particular event in Good Striker's life but it obviously meant a considerable amount to him – perhaps a favourite horse which died or was killed on the war trail.[21]

Above: A pipe-bag, probably Lakota, dating from c.1880. This is decorated with horse tracks in green, yellow, red and black, a wound motif in red and three cocoon-like elements. All these motifs fit well with Lakota symbology, mostly relating to prowess in the field of war. The emphasis here is almost certainly on the capturing of horses from the enemy. Cocoon motifs were said to have whirlwind associations and probably make reference to confusing the enemy in various encounters. The whole presentation relates to skill on the warpath. Not least, however, it is also a tribute to the skill of the craftswoman. With buckskin, sinew, beads and fringe, she has produced an article of beauty. (Courtesy Jim Strouse Collection, Golden, Colorado.)

Kin wanbli kayes´ yelo

("Even the eagle dies" - Lakota)

Winds
of Change

Below: *Natchez Indians surrounding a deer, depicted by the historian Le Page Du Pratz, c.1700. This required skilled band coordination.*

The highly effective and skillful hunting techniques developed by Native Americans were early commented on by white travelers and others. Thus, in the early 1700s when the French soldier and trader Etienne Veniard de Bourgemont traveled through the territory of Louisiana and beyond to the mouth of the Missouri, he observed the method of "surround" of wild game. This was a common hunting method used by the Native Americans before the coming of the horse. The hunters moved towards the game in line, then those on the extremities quickened their pace to curve the line and entrap the animals (see left). The "surround" was widespread and also used as an early warfare tactic. It was observed by Juan de Oñate in 1601 who recorded the annihilation of a Wichita(?) war-party on the Southern Plains.[1]

As the scholar Washburn observed, the advantage of such skilled and well coordinated tactics were recognized and adopted by

European military officers. In the conflicts with the Indians of New England in the seventeenth century (Chapter II), commanders such as Captain Benjamin Church of the Plymouth Colony modified the standard European formations. He spread his men when on the march "in the looser, more widely separated Indian fashion,... [they] learned how to move quickly and lightly through the forest and to utilize encirclement [of the enemy]." (Washburn, Trigger ed., 1978:99–100)

The ploy of decoy

Buffalo were difficult to kill with a bow and arrow by pedestrian hunters and ingenious techniques were developed to approach close enough for the kill. A type of "still hunt" was recorded by Catlin where stealthy hunters, covered in wolf skins, approached the herd. (p. 9) The "still hunt" was later used to devastating effect by white hunters armed with high powered rifles.

For aeons, however, the various tribes on the Plains employed the "pound" method to trap animals, vital to the nomads as a source of food and clothing.[2] Such hunting methods required carefully planned band coordination, often accompanied by days of ceremonial directed by a "divining man of known repute, who is believed to have the power of making the buffalo come into it by his enchantments." (Denig, 1930:532) Often human decoys were used to entice animals into the pound. These decoys had considerable skills: as one perceptive observer recorded, "there are but few among them who can do it... The person who brings the buffalo mounts a horse and meets them a great distance from camp. When within about 150 yards of the herd he covers his body with his robe, lies along the horse's back and imitates the bleating of a buffalo calf." (ibid)

Having caught the attention of the herd leaders, the decoy moves towards the mouth of the buffalo pound. He keeps downwind of the

Below: An early technique of hunting buffalo. This diorama at the "Head-Smashed-In" site in southern Alberta, is a depiction of a Blackfeet style Pishkun, or buffalo kill. Prior to the acquisition of the horse, the pedestrian nomads of the Plains commonly drove buffalo into V-shaped pounds, which terminated at a circular enclosure or at a cliff edge, as shown here. Such methods of hunting provided large quantities of meat and the inferior cuts were left to the wolves.

Above: *Confrontation! Engraving on an unusual style of pipe-tomahawk, showing a Woodland Indian threatening a white settler or trader. Dating from the early eighteenth century, the details of this scene are particularly interesting. Each man is shown wearing a distinctive form of headgear. The white with a hat, the Indian with a straight-up headdress, typical of the Woodland style. The tomahawk is of white manufacture; such weapons were used with great skill by the indigenous Indians.*

herd, renews the call of the calf and breaks his horse into a gallop. "The animals now take fright... [the decoy now veers off to one side] and the whole herd plunges madly down the precipice, one on top of the other, breaking their legs and necks in the fall." (ibid) As described earlier, similar techniques were used by the Subarctic people. (see Chapter II) They were also employed by the early inhabitants of the Great Plains—possibly ancestors of the Kutenai and Shoshone tribes—when hunting the vast herds of pronghorn antelope. (Grinnell, 1923)

The ploy of the decoy, often associated with enpounding within a natural or man-made barrier, was clearly an ancient skill in North America. Descriptions by the French explorer, Jacques le Moyne (c. 1550) in relation to the tribes of Florida, make reference to Timucua hunters disguised in deer hides. The hunters covered their heads using the hides as a mask to enable them to approach their quarry. Likewise in the 1640s, Samuel de Champlain described Huron hunters luring deer into a V-shaped trap, the subsequent actions being similar to those described in buffalo hunting nearly three centuries later.[3]

Decoys and camouflage in warfare

In April 1676, when the town of Sudbury (in present-day Massachusetts) was under siege during the "King Philip" War (Chapter II), highly successful ambushes were carried out on two English relief parties on a single day. Decoys were used to great effect: "a small number of Indian decoys lured them into the forest, where a waiting war party surrounded and badly mauled the company." (Malone, 1991:83) In such situations, as with deer and buffalo, the disguise matched the conditions; thus in forest combat, warriors sometimes camouflaged themselves from the waist upwards with green boughs. The colonial soldiers were described as unable to see the enemy and "yet felt their bullets out of the thick bushes where they lay in ambushment." (Gookin In Malone, 1991:88)

The "surround" by equestrian hunters

The Plains tribes employed two methods of hunting buffalo on horseback, the chase and surround. In the latter case, a large number of horsemen were required to ensure success; it was also a technique employed in warfare by the Plains tribes.

In 1833, whilst visiting the Minatarees (Hidatsa) on the Missouri River, the traveler George Catlin witnessed a buffalo surround. He left a graphic account: "The hunters... were all mounted on their "buffalo horses" and armed with bows and arrows or long lances, divided into two columns, taking opposite directions, and drew themselves gradually around the herd at a mile or more distance from them; thus forming a circle of horsemen at equal distances apart, who gradually closed in upon them with a moderate pace, at a signal given... In this grand turmoil (p.111) ...the hunters were galloping their horses around and driving the whizzing arrows, or their long lances to the hearts of these noble animals; ...[it was] a wild and desperate war... a desperate battle: and in the space of fifteen minutes, ...[there was] total destruction of the whole herd... [falling] before the destroying hands of mighty man." (Catlin, 1926 Vol I: 225–226)

The surround method eased the task of butchering, concentrating the animals in a relatively small killing field. It was, however, a dangerous technique because of the general mêlée of horse, man and buffalo in close proximity. The preferred method was the chase: a general rush by mounted hunters, each singling out a buffalo, riding alongside it and killing it at close quarters by skilled use of the bow, or lance.

Although the surround method was largely abandoned by the mid-nineteenth century, the equestrian skills needed—not least the effective use of weapons on horseback—were extended to the field of war. It was then described as "encirclement." (see p.117)[4]

Below: A buffalo "surround," as depicted by the artist and explorer George Catlin, in the summer of 1833. This was considered a dangerous technique, requiring nerve and great skill on horseback; horses and men were maimed or killed. Twenty years after Catlin recorded this scene, the "surround" was largely but a memory in the minds of the old-time hunters. The chase increasingly became a favored method, but that too required skilled use of the bow and horse.

Confrontation on the Plains

A slow war of suppression of the Plains Indian commenced with the shooting of an emaciated abandoned cow on the afternoon of August 18, 1854. The next day, despite the great diplomacy of both James Bordeaux (a white trader) and Conquering Bear, the Brulé chief, John L. Grattan and his entire command of almost thirty men were annihilated. The evidence suggests that ambuscade techniques were employed by both the Brulé and Oglala when it became apparent that diplomatic resolution was impossible.

The so-called "Grattan Massacre," as it became known, heralded the beginning of an increasingly bitter Indian-White confrontation on the Great Plains. The ways of war of the players were also markedly different—professional soldiers against village communities, superior resources and a heightened attitude of "Manifest Destiny" on one side. On the other, a brave and resourceful people attempting to maintain their freedom and lifestyle. They had, however, increasingly limited resources; not only in men and weaponry but also because of the depletion of the buffalo herds on which so much of their life depended. Warfare tactics, lifestyles and skills had to be markedly changed in order to survive the alien foe.[5]

"Savage warfare"

"Savage warfare was never more beautiful than in you. On you come, your swift, agile ponies springing down the winding ravine, the rising sun gleaming on your trailing war bonnets, on silver armlets, necklace, gorget; on brilliant painted shield and beaded legging; on naked body and beardless face, stained most vivid vermilion. On you come, lance and rifle, pennon and feather glistening in the rare morning light, swaying in the wild grace of your peerless horsemanship; nearer, till I mark the very ornament on your leader's shield. And on, too, all unsuspecting, come your helpless prey. I hold vengeance in my hand, but not yet to let it go. Five seconds too soon, and you can wheel about and escape us; one second too late, and

Below: *Huron warriors depicted in moosehair embroidery on birchbark, c.1860. Details of clothing, hairstyles, and footwear are shown. Such work was skillfully executed by the Huron women of Lorette. The scenes make reference to everyday activities, such as hunting, warfare and, as shown here, relaxation with a long-stemmed pipe. (Taylor Collection, Hastings, U.K.)*

my blue-coated couriers are dead men."
(King, 1890:36)

King was, perhaps somewhat romantically but with much realism, describing a typical clash between red and white as observed by so many military men on the Plains in the nineteenth century. A number of officers—such as Custer, Crook, Bourke and Miles—reported on the traditional war tactics and skills used by the Plains warrior: surprise and ambuscade, rapid mobility, admirable horsemanship and deft use of weapons as well as actions to keep their casualties to a minimum.

The following is such an account, witnessed by the Englishman, Dr William Bell who, in 1867, joined a government expedition to survey routes for a southern trans-continental railway. The terrain to be covered was a stretch from Fort Wallace, Kansas to Albuquerque on the Rio Grande. It was to cut through traditional hunting territory of the Southern Plains Indians and was bitterly opposed. In addition to insight into traditional war tactics of Arapaho, Cheyenne and Sioux, there are references to signalling techniques, war regalia and face paint, as well as the frightening brutality of the encounter.

During their surveying activities the expedition met up with Lieutenant George A. Custer's 7th Cavalry and Bell befriended a fellow Englishman, one Sergeant Frederick Wylyams, in Captain Albert Barnitz's G Troop of the Seventh Cavalry. Sergeant Wylyams was, according to Bell, a graduate of Eton who "while sowing his wild oats had made a fatal alliance in London and gone to grief." (Bell, 1869, Vol. I:46)

On Saturday June 22, 1867, a mixed band of Cheyenne, Arapaho and Sioux attacked Fort Wallace which was at that time considerably under strength, most troops having accompanied General W. S. Hancock on a treaty-making expedition to Fort Larned on the Santa

Above: Talahassee, a *Seminole leader, photographed c.1890. The tribe was involved in bitter disputes with the U.S. government c.1817–60. The major threat was removal from their traditional homelands to Indian Territory in present-day Oklahoma.*

111

Fe Trail. The attack was repulsed but it gave Bell his first opportunity to see "how the 'noble red men' fought." (ibid: 53) Following the short engagement on the 22nd, fifty soldiers under Captain Barnitz, including Sergeant Wylyams and Dr Bell, scouted in the vicinity of Fort Wallace. They were observed by a large war-party—four hundred or so in number. The leader was a tall warrior with a lance on a white horse "who was so conspicuous in the fight on Saturday." (ibid:59) The Indians signalled to one another by walking their horses in a circle, whilst the chief signalled to more distant warriors by means of a mirror "which flashed brilliantly in the sun." (ibid.)

No sooner had the cavalry followed the retiring band beyond the ridge, exchanging shots and skirmishing all the way than, on either flank, two fresh bodies of warriors suddenly appeared. They halted a few minutes when a powerful-looking warrior fancifully dressed, galloped along their front shouting suggestions; and then, like a whirlwind, with lances poised and arrows on the string, they rushed on the little band of fifty soldiers. The skirmishers fired and fell back on the line, and in an instant the Indians were amongst them. Now the tide was turned. Saddles were emptied, and the soldiers forced back over the ground towards the fort. The bugler fell, pierced by five arrows, and was instantly seized by a powerful warrior, who, stooping down from his horse, hauled him up before him, coolly stripped the body, and then, smashing the head of his naked victim with his tomahawk, threw him on the ground under his horse's feet. On the left of our line the Indians pressed heavily cutting off five men, amongst them Sergeant Frederick Wylyams. By this time it was more than evident that on horseback the soldiers were no match for the redskins. Most of them had never been opposed to Indians before; many were raw recruits; and their horses became so dreadfully frightened at the yells and the smell of the savages as to be quite unmanageable so Captain Barnitz gave the order to dismount.[6]

For two hours Capt. Barnitz waited with his thinned ranks for another advance of the Indians, but they prudently held back; and, after a prolonged consultation, retired slowly with their dead and

Above: *Souvenir of conflict in Minnesota (1862)—a tanned piece of Cut Nose's skin.*

Below: *The Santee Sioux leader Cut Nose, who was hanged at Mankato in 1862.*

wounded beyond the hills, to paint their faces black.

Aftermath

"I have seen in days gone by sights horrible and gory—death in all its forms of agony and distortion—but never did I feel the sickening sensation, the giddy, fainting feeling that came over me when I saw our dead, dying and wounded after this Indian fight. A handful of men, to be sure, but with enough wounds upon them to have slain a company, if evenly distributed. Sergeant Wylyams lay dead beside his horse and as the fearful picture first met my gaze, I was horror stricken. Horse and rider were stripped bare of trapping and clothes, while around them the trampled, blood-stained ground showed the desperation of the struggle." (ibid:59–61)

Identifying the war-party

According to Bell, the marks of the warriors from different tribes in this conflict were evident. Infuriated by the audacity of the surveying party these were designed to inspire fear as well as clearly state, by signs and symbols, exactly who the opposition were.[7]

"As I have said almost all the different tribes on the plains had united their forces against us, and each of these tribes has a different sign by which it is known."

"If we now turn to the body of poor Sergeant Wylyams, we shall have no difficulty in recognizing some meaning in the wounds. The muscles of the right arm, hacked to the bone, speak of the Cheyenne, or 'Cut Arms,' the nose slit denotes the 'Smaller tribe' or Arapaho; and the throat cut bears witness that the Sioux were also present."

Battle plans

As was discussed in Chapter II, intertribal warfare (as well as hunting) was frequently carefully

Below: A feat of horsemanship by a Sioux warrior, against bow-armed Shoshone, as depicted by the artist Alfred Jacob Miller, c.1837. Here, the warrior is dropping down behind his horse, using it as a shield. Such rapid movements confused the enemy. Such skillful tactics were effective against both the bow and musket, but less so against powerful rifles, which were progressively introduced in the 1860s.

planned and for the Plains tribes a war/hunting lodge was a recognized center of operations. (p.22)

There is good evidence, from Indian sources, which suggests that during the Indian-White confrontations of the nineteenth century some strategies and tactics were equally well planned.[8] Thus, some time prior to the so-called Fetterman Massacre, in December 1866, battle plans were discussed and rehearsed. Sioux and their Cheyenne allies, together with a few Arapaho, carefully marked out places of concealment some five miles northwest of Fort Phil Kearny (see map below). In addition to rehearsing an ambush, a decoy was used to simulate the approach of soldiers. This decoy, according to the Cheyenne informant White Elk, was a *Heemaneh'* or "half man and half woman." (Grinnell, 1956:237) In the rehearsal, the decoy approached the assembled Indians several times, and each time he reported more imaginary soldiers than previously. This was to emphasize to the assembled warriors that they were not to fire on a **few** soldiers but to wait for **many**—that would be the opportune time to attack.

On the night of December 20, the war chiefs sent ten warriors—six Sioux, two Cheyenne, and two Arapaho. to the vicinity of the Fort, as the first decoys.

Early on the morning of December 21, the warriors in the main camp[9] were directed by the chiefs to saddle up and make for Fort Phil Kearny. The scheme was to attack the wood train (which almost daily left the Fort) and so draw out a relief party from the Fort itself. The ten selected warriors would then act as decoys drawing the pursuers towards Peno Creek—the place previously selected so carefully for ambush. Here, Cheyenne and Arapaho were hidden on the upper-west-side, the Sioux to the south. They waited and "everyone kept very still."

Above: *Missionaries sought to convert tribes to a range of religions. Leaders such as Sitting Bull emphasized the sacredness of the Plains Indian calumet.*

Below: *Powder River country, c.1866. Shown here is Fort Phil Kearny, which initiated the "Sioux Wars" of the 1860s and 1870s.*

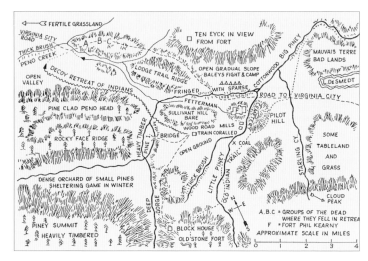

(ibid:239) Most of the warriors were armed with traditional weapons—bows, lances and war clubs—only a few had guns: old smooth-bore flintlocks.

The relief party, led by Captain William Fetterman, had in total eighty-one men, of which forty-eight were infantry armed with old Civil War Springfield muzzle-loading muskets, whilst twenty-seven cavalry had the new Spencer carbine.

White Elk explained to the historian, George Bird Grinnell, just how successful the decoys were. Fetterman, following the decoys, got as far as the Lodge Trail Ridge some three miles from the Fort. Here he hesitated, beyond the Ridge he could no longer be seen from the Fort. Decoys, however, caused him to order the whole command forward, the cavalry in the lead, the infantry following. The force was thus moving in weakened formation but there appeared to be little danger, with only the small group of Indians ahead of the command —the decoys! Near Peno Creek the decoy party suddenly split—a signal to spring the trap.

"When the charge was made, the sound of many hoofs made a noise like thunder and the soldiers began to fall back." (ibid:241) The entire command was annihilated. "All are dead... do not let even a dog get away." (ibid:243–244)

The strategy and attack had been successful. The entire command—eighty-one men—was, in the space of probably less than two hours, completely destroyed. However, the price was high. Those in the army command with fast-loading Spencer carbines—in particular, the two civilians Wheatley and Fisher, with Henry repeating rifles—wreaked havoc and more than fifty Sioux were killed. "The Sioux were laid out [after the battle] side by side and made two long rows, perhaps fifty or sixty men." (ibid:244) In terms of Plains Indian intertribal warfare, these were high casualties.[10]

The Indian victory signalled the beginning of the withdrawal of troops from the Powder River country.[11] However, the increasing sophistication of the opposition's weaponry was a telling demonstration of the lethal power of the gun. The frightening and decisive fire-power was further underlined at the Wagon Box encounter the following year.

Below: *Ridge Walker, a Northern Cheyenne scout, photographed at Fort Keogh, Montana, c.1890. By this time, guns were readily available to Indians and widely used for hunting purposes. The rifle carried by Ridge Walker appears to be a Model 1876 Winchester repeater, with an octagonal barrel.*

Bow and gun compared

As was discussed for the Woodlands, the Plains Indian was inexorably and progressively confronted by opponents whose mode of conduct in battle was markedly different to their own. Coupled with this, was the rapidly evolving technology of the gun. From the early matchlock, to musket, to carbine and finally the repeater rifle, tactics needed to change for survival. Guns were obtained by trade or theft but a reliable source was a continuing problem. As the historian Marie Sandoz, observed of Crazy Horse just before the Battle of the Rosebud, he "wished for guns, plenty of good rifles..."[12] (Sandoz, 1961:318)

In these fast changing times, not surprisingly both offensive and defensive warfare and hunting skills (as with the Woodland tribes some two centuries earlier (see Chapter II)) were increasingly modified. In most cases it obviously became a blend of traditional expertise and new technology; at times, however, as will be discussed, entirely new tactics and skills were demanded.

Some significant factors relating to a moving target and speed of the projectile—arrow, ball or bullet—are given in the Table below:

Below: *The Oglala Lakota Sioux, Makhpiya-lúta, or "Red Cloud," who bitterly opposed the encroachment into Powder River country in the 1860s. (from a painting by Frank Humphris)*

Table 1: Hitting a moving target with arrow and bullet

(a) Time to target

	Speed/ms^{-1}	Time/s (10m)	Time/s (100m)	Drop/m
Bow	30	0.3	3.3	50
Flintlock	150	0.1	1	2.5
Winchester	330	0.03	0.3	0.45

(b) Amount of movement across the line of fire:*

	At 10m	At 100m
Bow	4 m	40 m
Flintlock	1.3 m	13 m
Winchester	0.4 m	4 m

 * Taking speed of horse at 30 mph (approx. 13ms^{-1})

(c) Drop time for warrior using horse as shield:

Free fall of 1 meter = 0.45s

With downward pull = 0.25s (Estimate)

Thus, in the case of the bow, one can quite appreciate the early descriptions of Woodland warfare where there is reference to war-parties, some distance apart, who could actually dodge arrows fired by the opposition: similar action is implied by *Saukamappee* for early Plains warfare. (Chapter IV)

Such tactics would be less effective in the case of the flintlock; perhaps at the flash of ignition and at a distance of one hundred meters or more, a keen-eyed warrior could take action. But to a downward time of 0.25s should be added the reaction time of 0.7s. (Table 1) Time to target and time to drop (in order to use the horse as a shield) thus became comparable. So a flash-action tactic had its limitations and the technique alone would be useless against a Winchester. Increasingly, much of the equestrian skill associated with these tactics and so admired by artists, travelers and soldiers alike was, as will be discussed, largely made void by the rapid improvements in gun technology and its increasing availability.[13]

Above: *The popular Winchester rifle, Model 1873, and a fifty-round box of 0.44–40 caliber ammunition.*

Below: *The Lakota attempted to capture baby Kate Ballon, whose father was an officer at Fort Sidney, to help in their negotiations. They failed, and this coat was given to her as a sign of friendship. (Courtesy Museum, Sidney, Nebraska. Photograph by author.)*

Encirclement

The "surround" used in hunting the buffalo (p.109) had its counterpart in warfare. George Armstrong Custer, who knew the Plains tribes well on the field of war, referred to the tactic of "circling," as their "habitual manner of fighting... First the chiefs [lead] off, followed at regular intervals by the warriors, until the entire six or seven hundred were to be seen riding in single file as rapidly as their fleet-footed ponies could carry them. Preserving this order and keeping

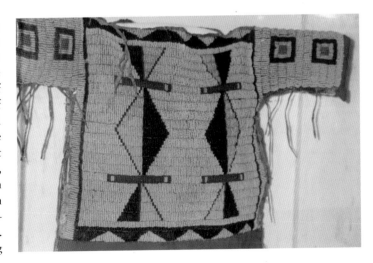

Left: *Comanche attacking a wagon train, as depicted by the artist Seth Eastman, in the mid-nineteenth century. Although a somewhat "classic" image, it was based on considerable factual evidence and illustrates the description by George Armstrong Custer of the Plains Indian war tactic of "circling." (see p. 117)*

up their savage chorus of yells... [they] envelop the train and escort, and make the latter appear like a small circle within a larger one. (Custer, Quaife ed., 1966:165) The circle was "gradually contracted" but the "full speed" of the ponies was maintained until the warriors were "sufficiently close to open fire upon the solders." Gait was "rapid... and in single file" presenting a confusing, difficult to hit opponent. (ibid.) Added to the problem of a fast-moving target was their "almost marvellous... horsemanship. Throwing themselves upon the sides of their well-trained ponies they left no part of their persons exposed to the aim of the troopers except the head and one foot." (ibid:166) Weapons were then aimed over or under the necks of the pony, the body of the animal acting as a shield.

Free drop behind the horse would take about 0.45s—quicker if there was a thrust downward by pulling on the saddle cinch. At one hundred meters or so this could be an effective maneuver against bow or musket by a keen-eyed warrior. With more modern weaponry — such as a Winchester—reaction time, plus drop time, compared with time to target, markedly narrowed. (Table 1) Even under these conditions, however, there is still the movement of a fast-moving equestrian warrior across the line of fire which would be several meters. Little wonder that Custer recorded "[the Indians] presented a most uncertain target." (ibid:165)

"They never fought again"

Courage, fine horsemanship and well tried battle tactics, however, increasingly met their match against gun-armed opponents. This was

Below: *Lakota (probably Oglala) warbonneted warrior, depicted on horseback, worked in beads on a traditional style of pipe-bag, c.1890. (Taylor Collection, Hastings, U.K.)*

dramatically demonstrated at the so-called "Wagon Box" encounter in August 1867.

After the disastrous Fetterman Massacre (see p.114) it was considered to be courting disaster to roam too far from the relative safety of the Fort. Wood, however, was continually required and contractors were employed to supply it. The contractors established a base for operations at Piney Island some six miles west of the Fort. In August 1867, these wood-cutters were guarded by an escort under the command of Captain James W. Powell. At about 7:30 am, a picket called out an alarm. Within a short time, some thirty men, including four civilians, were pinned down by a vastly superior force of Sioux (mainly Oglala under Red Cloud) and Cheyenne. They had, as their defence, a corral of fourteen wagon boxes, lifted off their running frames, since the latter were being used to haul the cordwood to the Fort.

So sure was Red Cloud of victory, that he allowed the women and children to witness the battle from the surrounding hills. The usual warfare skills and tactics were employed by the Sioux when facing gun-armed opponents under these circumstances. Whilst on horseback, first drawing the fire at a relatively safe distance, then "circling" at high speed and dropping behind the horse so presenting a confusing, difficult to hit, target. As the gun-fire reduced, the warriors closed in for the kill.[14]

Such tactics were effective against the early style of muzzleloader. It took some twenty seconds to reload; further, the average American soldier at this time was ineffective at about one hundred meters. (Boorman 2001:24)

Unknown to Red Cloud, however, was that in June 1867, some seven hundred breechloading Springfield rifles and a hundred thousand rounds of ammunition had arrived at the Fort. These new weapons were issued to the troops in July.

Below: *An Arikara scout, c.1880. Of particular interest is the saber in his left hand. These were important trade items. Many were surplus after the Napoleonic Wars (Hanson In Taylor, 2000:50); others were ordered direct from London or elsewhere. Although they were often carried as something of a status symbol, they were also used with great skill and to count coup on the battlefield.*

Below: A Nez Perce, or Kutenai gun-case, c.1890. Gun scabbards were essential items for protecting the weapon from excessive cold or moisture and were used at an early period. The Cree historian, Saukamappee, makes reference to their use in the mid-1700s. In the nineteenth century, they began to be increasingly decorated with beadwork. This piece is typical of the style—skillfully beaded at each end. (Robert Mucci Collection, Hastings, U.K.)

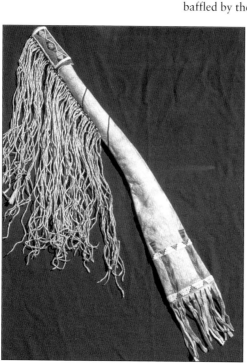

They completely replaced the older muzzleloading musket. Although, as with the muzzleloader, the Springfield had to be reloaded after each shot, the action only took about three seconds—some six to seven times faster than the muzzleloader. Additionally, this more modern weapon reduced the gun to target time by at least 50%. The rapidity with which the soldiers could reload and the accuracy of fire, confounded the Sioux-Cheyenne tactics: whatever the odds, it was now impossible to ride the enemy down before he could reload.

Various other tactics were tried. The grass was set fire, arrows were skillfully lofted into the corral some dropping almost vertically. Fire arrows were also used, tipped with a burning pitch, which stuck into the wooden wagon boxes.

Another mode of attack was adopted, this time on foot using the terrain as cover. But all to no avail; the Sioux were "completely baffled by the tremendous firepower they had experienced from what they believed was a small number of men in the corral." (Appleman, 1960:157)

In the ensuing engagement—which lasted nearly five hours—Red Cloud lost almost seventy of his best warriors and at least one hundred and twenty were wounded, some so severely that they were crippled for life. It was a turning point in the Lakota—Oglala in particular—stand against white domination.

Years later, Red Cloud recorded the psychological impact of a battle where improved gun technology devastated his forces and confounded the time-tested tactics. He reminisced that at the Piney Island, he had at his command over three thousand warriors "and lost over half;" when asked if he meant over fifteen hundred had been killed, he replied "I lost them. They never fought again." (Brady, 1905:58)

"Poisoned with blood" (Sitting Bull, 1877)
Although the Wagon Box fight proved such a disaster for the Lakota and their allies, Red Cloud did achieve his demands, which were first made in 1866. Then, he wanted a complete abandonment of the Forts

along the Bozeman Trail and a clear defining of the limits of the lands claimed by the Lakota. In April 1868, Peace Commissioners came to Fort Laramie and by November 1868 Fort Phil Kearny had been abandoned and burnt to the ground. Powder River country, and vast tracts of land east of the Big Horn Mountains, were defined as unceded Indian territory. An uneasy peace prevailed.

But the buffalo were disappearing rapidly. In 1872, for their hides alone—sometimes just their tongues—a million animals per year were slaughtered by white hunters. Many had high-powered rifles and employed the "still hunt" tactic. Professional hunters formed lines of camps along the banks of the Arkansas River and continuously shot buffalo, night and day as they came down to drink.

The Englishman, William Blackmore, reported on the carnage. They "frequently killed all that [they] wanted... from one stand." (Blackmore, In Taylor, 1975:108) Colonel Dodge reported on one hundred and twelve carcasses inside a semi-circle of some 200 yards radius, all of which had been killed by one man from the same spot in less than three-quarters of an hour." (Dodge In ibid.)

This was not the hunting/killing practice of the Plains tribes. The wanton slaughter appalled the Indians, not least Sitting Bull. "See the thousands of carcasses rotting on the Plains... What is this (?) ...the country there is poisoned with blood.[15] (ibid)

A new kind of war
As Crazy Horse reflected, when the new conflicts loomed in the mid-1870s, "this was a new kind of war that had come to the country...

Above: *George Armstrong Custer (1839–1876). Although best known for warring with Plains Indians, he also found much to admire in them: he noted, "the wonderful power and subtlety of his senses." (Custer, 1962:19)*

Below: *After the battle, June 25, 1876, painting by J.K. Ralston. Some unusual changes in warfare tactics, by the Lakota and Cheyenne, led to the demise of Custer and his immediate command.*

Above: *A Sioux burial tipi, c.1877. Structures such as this were used to hastily bury warriors killed in battle, generally cocooned in a buffalo robe, with their accoutrements of war.*

Right: *The Bear's Paw Battlefield as it is today. Situated in northern Montana, this was the site of the last stand of the Nez Perce Indians of Idaho, in October 1877. They finally capitulated after an almost two thousand mile journey from Idaho—just eighty miles from the Canadian border and freedom. Entrenchments on the battlefield by the Nez Perce were said to have been arranged with a skill that would have done credit to a military engineer. (Photograph by author.)*

not the old one of driving off a few raiding Snakes or Crows who made a little fighting between the time of the hunts and the other things of their lives. With the white warriors it was killing every day, killing all the time." (Sandoz, 1961:315)

Of professional soldiers against village communities, he said, they "do not seem to be men like you... they have no homes anywhere, no wives but the pay-women, no sons that they can know... We must fight them in a different way... not with the counting of many coups or doing great deeds to be told in the victory dance... make this a war of killing, a war of finishing, so we can live in peace in our own country." (ibid) The concept of Total War had finally reached the Plains Indian.

A clash with General George Crook's forces on the Rosebud on June 17, 1876, illustrated the departure from traditional battle tactics. Indian and other accounts make reference to battle plans on the part of the Lakota and their Cheyenne allies. Decoys were to be employed to draw the soldiers into ambush at an opportune moment in the Rosebud Canyon. To ensure surprise, the *akicita*[16] were put on guard, preventing any of the advancing warriors from prematurely attacking. That plan was ruined when Crook's Crow scouts discovered the "massed force of hostiles behind the hill." (Hyde, 1967:266)

Aware that Crook was intent on capturing the villages, the Indians took on the offensive. Instead of fleeing, the Sioux and Cheyenne charged "boldly and rapidly through the soldiers, knocking them from their horses with lances and knives, ...Part of the Sioux warriors broke through the line and swept around to Crook's rear." (ibid:264) They then reformed for a final "great charge" which would have probably overwhelmed the soldiers. Only the timely arrival of the cavalry—recalled by Crook after he had sent them to attack the villages—prevented what would have certainly been a disastrous clash.

Crook finally retreated to his base camp on Goose Creek where, for nearly six weeks, he awaited reinforcements. His "campaign was ruined and... he was kept pegged to his base camp while the hostiles were engaged with Custer." (ibid:265)

As one historian observed, the fight on the Rosebud marked a departure from the usual tactics of the Indians, "they exhibited unprecedented group impetuosity, courage, and persistence... They fought spiritedly on land removed from the immediate defense of their village... this kind of Indian warfare was almost unprecedented. The Plains Indians were not supposed to take the offensive." (Leermakers, 1960:234)

Just over a week later, similar tactics were used against Custer's forces. Reno, to his amazement, was met by an offensive, cohesive front of warriors as he charged the village in the valley of the Little Bighorn (Taylor, 1975): his retreat sealed Custer's fate.[17]

It proved, however, an empty victory. The buffalo were fast going and, after Custer, the army high command flooded the region with troops: they had too, plenty of guns.

The skills developed over aeons—both for the hunt and war—were now becoming increasingly meaningless. The bow was no match for the gun.

Above: *This may be the only extant photograph of the renowned war leader, Crazy Horse, perhaps taken at Fort Robinson in 1877. A skilled tactician, he urged a change in warfare tactics, which gave victory on both the Rosebud and the Little Bighorn in June 1876. (Courtesy Putt Thompson and Scott Burgan.)*

Endnotes

Chapter I

1. The most vulnerable part of a whale is just behind its head. The harpoon passed through the flesh and penetrated several feet into the blubber then, ideally, pierced the heart or lungs.

2. The buffalo dance of the Missouri River tribes (see pp.17 & 32), illustrates this point.

3. The stormy petrel was one spiritual helper particularly sought by the Nootka hunter. Another was the spirit of the whale itself.

4. This is but one example. Others are buffalo hunts, seal hunts, caribou drives and the like. All demanded, of course, special skills as well as courage and tenacity.

5. As with the Plains and Woods buffalo, there were two types of caribou, the barren ground caribou, *Rangifer articus*, and the woodland, *Rangifer caribou*.

6. In the historic period, the Chipewyan occupied the region west of Hudson Bay. The winters in this region are long and severe. The caribou was essential to their survival.

7. In particular, caribou meat was generally wind-dried, smoked in strips, or pounded into a powder, and then stored for future use.

8. I am exceedingly grateful to the late J.G.E. Smith of the Museum of the American Indian, New York, for relating to me several episodes of Chipewyan life.

9. Archeological evidence from the Central and Northern Plains verifies the numerous traditions of the great antiquity of eagle trapping. (See Bowers, 1950 and 1965, for a discussion of this in some detail)

10. The Pueblo in the Southwest, the Virginia Indians and the New England Narragansett for example.

11. Even the smaller black bear could sustain many bullet wounds: "enough to kill almost any other animal, will produce little effect at first on the black bear…" (Berlandier, Eweres ed., 1969:46)

12. The famous Blackfeet chief, Crowfoot, speared and killed a huge grizzly single-handed. It brought him fame; from that time on, "he was recognized throughout the tribe as a prominent chief."

(Dempsey, 1972:54)

13. Inflicting all possible damage on the enemy and excessive killing was largely alien to Indian warfare.

14. (Fraser Pakes to C.T., December 2002) Pakes' observations relating to Native American militarism, both in his publications (1968 and 1989) and in correspondence, helped considerably in the formulation of my own opinions on this fascinating subject.

15. The fur trade caused an enhancement of warring of the Huron by the Iroquois, who had always been traditional enemies. A policy of Total War—complete destruction—was pursued by the Iroquois against some twenty Huron villages.

16. In c.1650, some twenty Huron villages had an estimated population of twenty thousand. By 1905, the total number of Huron had dropped to less than one thousand.

17. The site of Fort McKenzie is now on private land. It is ten miles south of Fort Benton in present-day northern Montana.

18. In most Indian conflicts, heroic efforts were made to rescue the body of a fallen comrade.

19. As with vision quest sites, war lodges have been progressively destroyed over the years, by the ravages of time—natural deterioration, fire, vandalism.

20. In this context, the reader's attention is drawn to the description of Huron and Algonquian war leaders, c.1600, rehearsing war tactics
(See Chapter II)

Chapter II

1. Chief Black Hawk (c.1812), summed up the difference between White and Indian tactics. The former, regardless of the numbers lost, the latter keeping losses to a minimum. (Benn, 1998:167)

2. Citing Champlain, Malone (1991:21) concluded that tactical planning and rehearsal was probably common throughout the Eastern Woodlands. See Chapter VI for the Plains tribes.

3. Fletcher makes reference to the appointment of two lieutenants, or "little leaders," to act in the

leader's place in the event of his death. (Fletcher In Hodge ed., Vol.II, 1910:915)

4. Although avoiding danger when cornered, as with warriors, the male turkey was a very formidable opponent.

5. Alderman—the Indian who acquired Metacom's hand—was said to have earned "many a penny" by putting it on exhibit. (Lepore, 1998:173)

6. Retreat in Indian warfare was common. It was considered prudent to conserve lives in a society where population was so small.

7. These skills were acquired in hunting and games. (Benn, 1998:70)

8. Note the grisly souvenir sold after the hanging of the Sioux chief, Cut Nose (see introduction). Both episodes a white custom!

9. One interpretation of the tribal name Mohawk was "man-eaters." (Hewitt In Hodge ed., Vol.I, 1907:921)

10. Although Woodland peoples were not nomads, they did make seasonal moves with little difficulty. (Malone, 1991:11)

11. In Hewitt's opinion, the acquisition of firearms—from the Dutch—by the Iroquois, was an "important factor" in their eventual successes against the Huron who had few guns. (Hewitt In Hodge ed., Vol.II, 1910:588)

12. Only one bow of Indian make and from the mid-seventeenth century, now exists. This is the so-called Sudbury bow. It is now in the collections of the Peabody Museum, Harvard University.

13. Indians appear to have quickly seen the advantage of the flintlock over the matchlock. More so than the Governors of the various White colonies in eastern North America.

14. Considering the Indian style of warfare in eastern North America, it is clear that the tomahawk was considered a prime weapon for use at close contact—and superior to the knife. (Peterson, 1971:24)

15. "Tomahawk" perhaps derives from the Delaware *tomahakan* and the Mahican *tumnahecan*. (Taylor, 2001:30)

16. The Mohawk were the most prominent of the Iroquoian tribes.

Mohawk was often used as a synonym for the confederation.

Chapter III

1. There were, however, others with "flat occiput, flat nose, open nostrils, thin, everted lips and projecting chins… there seem to be two distinct classes among them." (Bourke, 1891:123)

2. This scalp is now in the Great Yarmouth Museum, Norfolk, U.K. An accompanying letter, dated 1864, gives details of its acquisition. (Taylor, 2000:26, illustration)

3. The lack of suitable forage and the rough terrain through which an Apache hunter or warrior customarily traveled, clearly worked against extensive use of the horse.

4. The mound of earth thrown up by the field-rat located its habitation. This had a number of entrances. Aware of this, Apache hunters partially blocked the main entrance with a curved stick and prodded through the others. The escaping field-rat generally partially emerged—cautious of any outside danger—with its body across the stick. A quick, skillful move by the Apache broke the back of the rodent. (Bourke, 1891:129–130)

5. Research suggests that both the scratch stick and drinking straw were widespread, not only in North America but throughout the world. Traditionally, at least, they were always associated with ritualistic or ceremonial ideas.

6. There are references to meteorological phenomena in the acquisition of supernatural powers. One Medicine Man with "star power" was said to impart skillful use of the gun in both hunting and war. (Goodwin, Basso ed., 1971:273)

7. As with the tactics of the Woodland tribes discussed in Chapter II, it is clear that the Apache considered that they were far more effective—and had a far better chance of survival—than when they were moving in compact bodies.

8. *Hoddentin* was also offered to the Great Bear and Morning Star. Typical prayers were appeals for survival.

Chapter IV

1. Of course, the most important of the Plains animals was the buffalo which roamed in vast herds. In early days, c.1700, buffalo were found as far east as Virginia and North Carolina.
2. Plains Indian Religion—the "Oneness of All Things" as Black Elk put it—is discussed in ibid:60-89. Attention is drawn to the Lakota's *Tobtob Kin*, which embraced the physical and spiritual aspects of the world. (ibid:61-62)
3. In September, 1800, the North West Company trader, Alexander Henry, recorded that the Plains just west of the Red River, were covered with buffalo as far as the eye could see.
4. For the changing climatic conditions and the impact on the indigenous population, which obviously included hunting and warfare, see Owsley and Jantz eds., 1994:11-12.
5. Archeological evidence suggests that scalping was a prehistoric practice, "having great antiquity in the Northern Plans" (Hollimon and Owsley in ibid:351).
6. Women and dogs were the main burden-bearers prior to the advent of the horse. In c.1720, the French trader and soldier, Bourgmont, referred to loads of up to 300 lbs. (approxiamately 140 kg.) being carried by women.
7. Three shields found in a cave in Utah in 1925 and having Plains Indian characteristics, were just over 3 ft (1m) in diameter.
8. For more details on the horse and body armor by Plains tribes, see Ewers (1955), Taylor (2001).
9. Similar techniques were used in the hunt, such as the Natchez surround of wild game, referred to by Le Page Du Pratz (see Introduction and Chapter I).
10. The Spanish suppressed the sale of guns to Indians in the Southwest. In contrast, tribes in the Northeast obtained guns so as to contribute to the lucrative fur trade. This is discussed in more detail in Chapter V.
11. The scholar, Åke Hultkrantz, is of the opinion that pedestrian Shoshone made extensive use of the Plains resources, for thousands of years (see Sturtevant and Taylor, 1991:126-127).
12. Gun covers were essential in cold and damp. This is one of the earliest references to the use of gun-cases by the Plains tribes.
13. In 1810, superior gun-armed Flathead, defeated the Blackfeet (Piegan). An infantry battle pattern was adopted by the Flathead in this encounter, because "fire from afoot [with muskets] was far more accurate than fire from horseback" (Secoy, 1966:53).
14. With more horses becoming available, the trade in women as burden-bearers progressively reduced.
15. The horse was shot through the muscular part of the neck, just above the vertebrae. The wound, which apparently healed quickly, paralysed the animal for a few minutes.
16. The former dominant tribe on the Southern Plains—the Apache—were displaced by the Comanche-Caddoan alliance, c.1750. At this time, the Caddoans were beginning to obtain a few guns from the French to the east.
17. There is evidence of some fluctuations of the supply of guns and ammunition to the Comanche. In the 1720s, it appears that they did have sufficient arms (obtained from the French), to drive the Apache from their *rancherias*. However, from about 1750, French traders withdrew. It was not until almost a generation later, that the trade was resumed. (See Hyde, 1959:146-150 for an interesting discussion relating to this trade and his clear references to the decisive impact that guns had on the balance of power between tribes in the region).

Chapter V

1. (a) The Dutch were very active in trading guns to the Iroquois as early as 1645 (Hamilton, 1980:9). (b) The Northwest trade gun was very popular on the Northern Plains.
2. Dogs as beasts of burden, could be troublesome. Not only were they meat-eaters, but they could be very unruly! (See Ewers, 1955:306-307).
3. Horses bred by the Plateau tribes and the Crow Indians, were considered amongst the best by Blackfeet horse raiders.
4. At the Beecher Island of September 1868. Roman Nose had no time to go through the purification ceremony. He was subsequently shot in the back by Forsyth's scouts and died shortly after.
5. I have discussed the use of maps (including one produced by the Cheyenne, Little Robe, and now in the British Museum, London) in Taylor, 1994 (169-172).
6. The fascinating aspect of pictographic messages and the seemingly universal understanding, is discussed in ibid:(172-175). In this respect, it may be likened to the Sign Language.
7. Over the last thirty years or so, I have visited several such lodges in the remoter parts of Montana, Wyoming and North Dakota.
8. A shirt, which was formerly in The Wet's possession, is now in the Field Museum of Natural History, Chicago (specimen number 69417).
9. It is of interest to note that the name "Woman Chief" was widely used by Plains Indians, for those women who were successful in warfare (see Weist in Wood and Liberty, eds., 1980:263).
10. More recent, extensive data, indicates that the Plains tribes were far more skillful and innovative in the production of riding equipment—both functional and decorative—than Clark Wissler's earlier studies (1915) suggest.
11. This saddle and associated accoutrements, with bone toggles and hair cintures, are unusual. The combination particularly caught the attention of the late Norman Feder of the Denver Art Museum. (Liverpool specimen number 1956:25:864).
12. Sitting Bull's lance has been described as being 7 or 8 feet (approx. 2.2m) long and tipped with an 8 inch (20cm) long notched iron blade (Utley, 1993:19). Sitting Bull apparently wielded this weapon with masterly skill.
13. The method is well illustrated in a sketch by the Peigan artist, Calvin Boy (Ewers, 1955:201.Fig.29).
14. The majority of pipe tomahawks seem to have been produced more as a "cottage type" industry, rather than, as in the case of knives, on a production line.
15. The Blackfeet informant, *Saukamappee*, describes Shoshone warriors on horseback, the dextrous handling of their stone-headed clubs, causing havoc amongst the Peigans.
16. Although the tomahawk was generally used in the same manner as a club it was, on occasions, thrown—sometimes with masterly skill (as discussed in the text).
17. This observation is based on a discussion with Graeme Rimer, Keeper of Weapons at the Royal Armouries, Leeds, UK (June 1999).
18. The Californian tribes and the Paiute employed very short sinew-backed bows, although neither group used the horse.
19. For typical pictographs, see Taylor (1998:68).
20. It is of interest to note that Captain Lewis, on the famous Lewis and Clark expedition of 1803-1806, carried a saber as a signal of his office.
21. Good Striker's war exploits are documented on the pictographic panels in the Fort Macleod Museum in southern Alberta.

Chapter VI

1. Some fifteen hundred Plains Apache encompassed the Wichita. *Saukamappee* related similar tactics for the Northern Plains. (Chapters IV and V)
2. The termination of the pound was a cliff edge or large circular enclosure.
3. The known fact that the scent of humans causes panic amongst animals was, it appears, often used to good effect and was a part of Indian hunting skills.
4. Of the surround method—which required so much skill—Ewers commented: "Certainly the best contemporary descriptions of [the surround] are found in writings of the period ante-1850." (Ewers, 1995:155)
5. Many Indian-White confrontations on the Plains involved village communities, which compounded the problem of the warriors when attacked.
6. The dismounted cavalry were described as pouring "a well-directed volley from their Spencers, the Indians for the first time wavered." (Bell, 1869, Vol.I:59)
7. Bell gives some interesting observations here, relating to the use of the sign language to identify vari-

ous Plains tribes. (ibid)

8. This is a topic that, to date, has received scant attention by scholars. The following discussion deserves fuller attention than can be given here.

9. The Sioux and Cheyenne villages were on the Tongue River, thirty miles north of Fort Phil Kearny.

10. The fact that Indian males were the main providers, as well as protectors, of both family and community, led to great emphasis on keeping casualties to a minimum.

11. An extended investigation, ordered by the then President, Andrew Johnson, led to this notable withdrawal almost certainly because it was conceded that it was in violation of existing treaty agreements. (See Taylor, 1975:102)

12. As with the Woodland tribes (Chapter II), some individuals were adept at recycling guns: "Good Hand... knew how to make them work very well, even those the soldiers had broken whipping their horses." (Sandoz, 1961:322)

13. See Boorman (2001:30–49), the Chapter "The Guns that won the West."

14. Custer makes reference to the "war pony:" "the favorite of the herd, fleet of foot, quick in intelligence, and full of courage." (Custer, 1962:200)

15. Sitting Bull, together with some one thousand followers, retreated to Canada in March 1877. He ultimately surrendered at Fort Buford in July 1881. (See Taylor, 1975:121)

16. The *akicita* is Lakota for a head warrior or a policeman who had responsibility for maintaining camp order.

17. The Battle of the Little Bighorn, June 25, 1876.

Bibliography

Afton, Jean, David Fridtjof Halaas, Andrew E. Masich
1997 *Cheyenne Dog Soldiers.* Niwot, CO: University Press of Colorado.

Albers, P., B. Medicine
1983 *The Hidden Half: Studies of Plains Indian Women.* Washington, DC: University Press of America.

Appleman, Roy E.
1960 The Wagon Box Fight. *Great Western Indian Fights.* Allred, Dykes, Goodwyn & Simms eds., pp148–62 New York, NY: Doubleday & Company Inc.

Bell, W.
1869 *New Tracks in North America.* 2 Vols. London.

Benn, Carl
1998 *The Iroquois in the War of 1812.* Toronto, Buffalo, London: University of Toronto Press.

Berlandier, J. Louis
1969 *The Indians of Texas in 1830.* John C. Ewers, ed. Washington, DC: Smithsonian Institution Press.

Bishop, Morris
1949 *Champlain: The Life of Fortitude.* London: Macdonald.

Blish, Helen H.
1967 *A Pictographic History of the Oglala Sioux.* Lincoln, NE: University of Nebraska Press.

Bohr, Roland
1996 *Plains Indian Archery Gear of the Historic Period.* Seminar Paper. Bismark, ND: University of North Dakota.

Boorman, Dean K.
2001 *The History of Winchester Firearms.* London: Salamander Books Ltd.

Bourke, John G.
1891 *On The Border With Crook.* New York, NY: Charles Scribner's Sons.
1892 The Medicine-men of the Apache. *9th Annual Report of the B.A.E. 1887–1888.* pp.443–595. Washington, DC: Smithsonian Institution.
1993 *Apache Medicine-men.* New York, NY: Dover Publications, Inc., Reprint. (First published 1892)

Bowers, Alfred W.
1950 *Mandan Social and Ceremonial Organization.* Chicago, IL: The University of Chicago Press.
1965 *Hidatsa Social and Ceremonial Organization.* Bulletin 194 of the B.A.E. Washington, DC: Smithsonian Institution.

Brady, Cyrus Townsend
1905 *Indian Fights and Fighters.* New York, NY: McClure, Phillips & Co.

Catlin, George
1841 *Letters and Notes on the Manners, Customs, and Condition of the North American Indians.* 2 Vols. London: Published by author.
1926 *North American Indians.* 2

Vols. Edinburgh: John Grant.

Clark, Capt. W.P.
1885 *The Indian Sign Language.* Philadelphia, PA: L.R. Hamersly & Co.

Custer, General George A.
1962 *My Life on the Plains.* Norman, OK: Oklahoma Press.
1966 *My Life on the Plains.* Milo Milton Quaife, ed. Lincoln, NE: University of Nebraska Press. (Reprint)

Dedera, Don
1971 Is Geronimo Alive and Well in the South Vietnamese Central Highlands? *Mankind Magazine.*

Dempsey, Hugh A.
1972 *Crowfoot Chief of the Blackfeet.* Norman, OK: University of Oklahoma Press.

Denig, Edwin Thompson
1930 Indian Tribes of the Upper Missouri. J.N.B. Hewitt, ed. *Forty-sixth Annual Report of the B.A.E.* pp.375–628. Washington, DC: Smithsonian Institution.

Densmore, Frances
1913 *Chippewa Music—II.* Bulletin 53 of the B.A.E. Washington, DC: Smithsonian Institution.
1918 *Teton Sioux Music.* Bulletin 61 of the B.A.E. Washington, DC: Smithsonian Institution.

De Vries, David P. See Vries, David P. de

Dodge, Richard I.
1877 *The Plains of the Great*

West. New York, NY.

Eckert, Allan W.
1992 *A Sorrow in our Heart: The Life of Tecumseh.* New York, NY: Bantam Books.

Ewers, John C.
1955 *The Horse in Blackfoot Indian Culture.* Bulletin 159 of the B.A.E. Washington, DC: Smithsonian Institution.
1968 *Indian Life on the Upper Missouri.* Norman, OK: University of Oklahoma Press.
1975 Intertribal Warfare as the Precursor of Indian-White Warfare on the Northern Great Plains. *The Western Historical Quarterly.* (Reprint). Vol.VI, No.4.
1994 Women's Roles in Plains Indian Warfare. *Skeletal Biology in the Great Plains.* Douglas W. Owsley and Richard L. Jantz, eds. pp.325–332. Washington, DC: Smithsonian Institution.

Fletcher, Alice C., Francis La Flesche
1911 The Omaha Tribe. *27th Annual Report of the B.A.E.* Washington, DC: Smithsonian Institution.

Friederici, Georg
1907 Scalping in America. *Smithsonian Report for 1906.* pp.423–438. Washington, DC: Government Printing Office.

Bibliography

Gilman, Carolyn, Mary Jane
Schneider
1987 *The Way to Independence.*
St. Paul, MN: Minnesota
Historical Society Press.
Goodwin, Grenville
1971 *Western Apache Raiding
and Warfare.* Keith H. Basso, ed.
Tuscon, AZ: The University of
Arizona Press.
Greene, Jerome A.
1994 *Lakota and Cheyenne
Indian Views of the Great Sioux
War, 1876–1877.* Norman, OK:
University of Oklahoma Press.
Grinnell, George Bird
1920 *When Buffalo Ran.* New
Haven: Yale University Press
1923 *The Cheyenne Indians:
Their History and Ways of Life.* 2
Vols. New Haven: Yale University
Press.
1956 *The Fighting Cheyennes.*
Norman, OK: University of
Oklahoma Press.

Hamilton, T.M.
1980 *Colonial Frontier Guns.*
Chadron, NE: The Fur Press.
Hardorff, Richard G.
1995 *Cheyenne Memories of the
Custer Fight.* Lincoln, NE and
London: University of Nebraska
Press.
Henry, Alexander, David
Thompson
1897 *New Light on the Early
History of the Greater Northwest.
The manuscript journals of
Alexander Henry and David
Thompson 1799–1814.* 3 Vols.
Elliott Coues, ed. New York, NY:
Francis P. Harper.
Hodge, Frederick Webb, ed.
1907–1910 *Handbook of
American Indians North of
Mexico.* 2 Vols. Washington, DC:
Smithsonian Institution. (Reprint:
1965 New York, NY: Rowman
and Littlefield).
Hough, Walter
1893 *Primitive American Armor.*
Washington, DC: Smithsonian
Institution.
Howard, James H., ed.
1996 *Lakota Warrior: Joseph
White Bull.* Lincoln, NE and
London: University of Nebraska
Press, Bison Books.
Hyde, George E.
1937 *Red Cloud's Folk.* Norman,
OK: University of Oklahoma
Press

1959 *Indians of the High Plains:
From the Prehistoric Period to the
Coming of Europeans.* Norman,
OK: University of Oklahoma
Press.

Innis, Harold A.
1930 *Peter Pond Fur Trader and
Adventurer.* Toronto

Jablow, Joseph
1950 *The Cheyenne in Plains
Indian Trade Relations
1795–1840.* Seattle, WA and
London: University of Washington
Press.

Kenton, Edna, ed.
1956 *Black Gown and Redskins.*
London, New York, NY, and
Toronto: Longmans, Green and
Co.
King, Charles
1890 *Campaigning With Crook
and Stories of Army Life.* New
York, NY: Harper & Brothers.
King, J.C.H.
1991 *Woodlands Artifacts From
the studio of Benjamin West
1738–1820. American Indian Art*
magazine. pp.34–47. Scottsdale,
AZ.
Kinietz, W. Vernon
1940 *The Indians of the Western
Great Lakes, 1615–1760.
Occasional Contributions.* No.10.
Ann Arbor, MI: Museum of
Anthropology, University of
Michigan.
Kurz, Rudolph
1937 *Journal of Rudolph
Friederich Kurz.* J.N.B. Hewitt,
ed. Washington, DC: Smithsonian
Institution.

La Verendrye, P.G.V.
1927 *Journals and Letters of
Pierre Gaultier de Varennes de la
Verendrye and his Sons.* Lawrence
J. Burpee, ed. Publication 16.
Toronto: Champlain Society.
Leermakers, J.A.
1960 *The Battle of the Rosebud.
Great Western Indian Fights.*
Allred, Dykes, Goodwyn &
Simms eds. pp.225–34. New
York, NY: Doubleday &
Company, Inc.
Lepore, Jill
1998 *The Name of War. King
Philip's War and the Origins of
American Identity.* New York,
NY: Alfred A. Knopf, Inc.

Lewis, Oscar
1942 *The Effects of White
Contact upon Blackfoot Culture.*
Centennial Anniversary
Publication, The American
Ethnological Society 1842–1942.
Seattle, WA: University of
Washington Press.
Malone, Patrick M.
1991 *The Skulking Way of War.*
New York, NY and Oxford:
Madison Books.
Mark, Joan
1988 *A Stranger in her Native
Land. Alice Fletcher and the
American Indians.* Lincoln, NE
and London: University of
Nebraska Press.
Marquis, Thomas B.
1931 *Wooden Leg. A Warrior
Who Fought Custer.* Lincoln, NE:
University of Nebraska Press.
Mishkin, Bernard
1966 *Rank and Warfare Among
the Plains Indians.* Seattle, WA
and London: University of
Washington Press.
McCracken, Harold
1957 *The Beast That Walks Like
Man.* London: Oldbourne Press.
McKenney and Hall
1972 *The Indian Tribes of North
America.* 3 Vols. Frederick Webb
Hodge, ed. Totowa, NJ: Rowman
and Littlefield. (First published
1836).

Nadeau, Gabriel
1938(?) *Indian Scalping:
Technique in Different Tribes.*
Rutland, MA: Rutland State
Sanatorium.

Opler, Morris E., Harry Hoijer
1940 *The Raid and Warpath
Language of the Chiricahua
Apache. American
Anthropologist.* 42:617–634.
Owsley, Douglas W., Richard L.
Jantz, eds.
1994 *Skeletal Biology in the Great
Plains.* Washington, DC and
London: Smithsonian Institution.

Pakes, Fraser J.
1968 *The 'No-Flight' Societies of
the Plains Indians. The English
Westerners' Brand Book.*
Vol.10,No.4. London.
1989 *Making War Attractive. The
English Westerners' Brand Book.*
Vol.26,No.2. London.

Peterson, Harold L.
1957 *American Knives.* New
York, NY: Charles Scribner's Sons.
1971 *American Indian
Tomahawks.* New York, NY:
Museum of the American Indian,
Heye Foundation. (First published
1965)
Peterson, Jacqueline, Laura Peers
1993 *Sacred Encounters.* The De
Smet Project, Washington State
University. Norman, OK, and
London: University of Oklahoma
Press.
Porter, Joseph C.
1986 *Paper Medicine Man: John
Gregory Bourke and his American
West.* Norman, OK, and London:
University of Oklahoma Press.

Sandoz, Mari
1961 *Crazy Horse: The Strange
Man of the Oglalas.* Lincoln, NE:
University of Nebraska Press.
(First published 1942).
Secoy, Frank Raymond
1966 *Changing Military Patterns
on the Great Plains.* Seattle, WA:
University of Washington. (First
published 1953).
Smith, DeCost
1943 *Indian Experiences.*
Caldwell, ID: The Caxton Printers
Ltd.
Smith, James G.E.
1978 Economic Uncertainty in an
'Original Affluent Society':
Caribou and Caribou Eater
Chipewyan Adaptive Strategies.
Arctic Anthropology 15 (1).
pp.68–88.
1981 Chipewyan. *Handbook of
North American Indians.* Vol.6
Subarctic. June Helm, ed.
pp.271–284. Washington, DC:
Smithsonian Institution.
Smith, Marian W.
1938 The War Complex of the
Plains Indians. *Proceedings of the
American Philosophical Society,*
Vol.78. No.3.
Stone, William L.
1864 *Life of Joseph Brant
(Thayendanegea).* 2 Vols. Albany.
Sturtevant, William C., Colin F.
Taylor.
1991 *The Native Americans.*
London: Salamander Books Ltd.

Taylor, Colin
1975 *The Warriors of the Plains.*
London: The Hamlyn Publishing
Group.

1994 *The Plains Indians*. London: Salamander Books Ltd.
1997 *North American Indians*. Bristol: Parragon.
1998 *Buckskin & Buffalo: The Artistry of the Plains Indians*. London: Salamander Books Ltd.
2000 *Hoka Hey! Scalps to Coups: The Impact of the Horse on Plains Indian Warfare*. Bilingual. Wyk auf Foehr, Germany: Tatanka Press. Verlag für Amerikanistik.
2001 *Native American Weapons*. London: Salamander Books Ltd. and Norman, OK: University of Oklahoma Press.
Thomas, Davis, Karin Ronnefeldt, eds.
1976 *People of the First Man*. New York, NY: E.P. Dutton & Co., Inc.
Thompson, David
1916 *David Thompson's Narrative of his Explorations in*

Western America, 1784–1812. J.B. Tyrrell, ed. Toronto
Trigger, Bruce G.
1969 *The Huron. Farmers of the North*. New York, NY et al: Holt, Rinehart and Winston.

Utley, Robert M.
1993 *The Lance and The Shield: The Life and Times of Sitting Bull*. New York, NY: Ballantine Books.

Vries, David P. de
1909 *Narratives of New Netherland 1609–1644*. J. Franklin Jameson, ed. New York, NY: Charles Scribner's Sons. (Reprint: New York, NY: Barnes and Noble, 1967).

Wallace, Ernest, E. Adamson Hoebel
1952 *The Comanches: Lords of*

the South Plains. Norman, OK: University of Oklahoma Press.
Washburn, Wilcomb E.
1978 Seventeenth-Century Indian Wars. *Handbook of North American Indians*. Vol.15 Northeast. Bruce G. Trigger, ed. pp.89–100. Washington, DC: Smithsonian Institution.
Webb, Walter Prescott
1931 *The Great Plains*. New York, NY: Grosset & Dunlop.
Wedel, Waldo R.
1961 *Prehistoric Man on the Great Plains*. Norman, OK: University of Oklahoma Press.
Weist, Katherine M.
1980 Plains Indian Women: An Assessment. *Anthropology on the Great Plains*. Lincoln, NE and London: University of Nebraska Press.
Wildschut, William

1960 *Crow Indian Medicine Bundles*. John C. Ewers, ed. New York, NY: Museum of the American Indian, Heye Foundation.
Wissler, Clark
1907 Some Protective Designs of the Dakota. *A.M.N.H.* Vol.I, Part II. pp.19–53. New York, NY.
1911 Social Organization and Ritualistic Ceremonies of the Blackfoot Indians. *A.M.N.H.* Vol.VII, Part I. New York, NY.
1915 Riding Gear of the North American Indians. *A.M.N.H.* Vol.17, Part I. New York, NY.
Wood, W. Raymond, Margot Liberty, eds.
1980 *Anthropology on the Great Plains*. Lincoln, NE and London: University of Nebraska Press.

Picture Credits